W9-DCA-865

THE
BOOK
OF THE
BIBLE

BY MARK LITTLETON

TESTAMENT
BOOKS

This 2001 edition is published by Testament Books™,
an imprint of Random House Value Publishing, Inc.
280 Park Avenue, New York, NY 10017
by arrangement with Ottenheimer Publishers, Inc.
5 Park Center Court, Suite 300, Owings Mills, MD 21117.

Testament Books™ and design are trademarks of
Random House Value Publishing, Inc.

Random House
New York • Toronto • London • Sydney • Auckland
http://www.randomhouse.com/

Printed and bound in the United States of America.

A catalog record for this title is available from the Library of Congress.

ISBN: 0-517-16406-X

9 8 7 6 5 4 3 2 1

CONTENTS

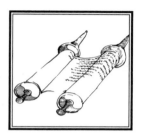

WHAT IS THIS BOOK WE CALL THE BIBLE?

Martin Luther said, "The Bible is alive, it speaks to me; it has feet, it runs after me; it has hands, it lays hold on me."

Abraham Lincoln felt so strongly about its importance that he said, "I believe the Bible is the best gift that God has ever given to man. All the good from the Savior of the world is communicated to us through this Book. I have been driven to my knees by the overwhelming conviction that I had nowhere else to go."

The great cinematographer, Cecil B. DeMille, was once asked why he produced so many movies about the Bible. He said, "Why let two thousand years of publicity go to waste!"

The Bible has a diverse and powerful impact. It is simple, but sublime; flawless, yet full of people with flaws. It tells us how to live, and it declares that it has God's life in its very words. It convicts us of sin, offers us hope of forgiveness, and promises heavenly rewards for those who will take its words with gravity and faith.

Our word "Bible" comes from the Greek word, *biblia,* which means "books." People in those days used "biblia" to refer to many different kinds of books. But when it comes to the Bible, there is only one! It is the Book of Books much like Jesus is called the King of Kings, and God the Lord of Lords. Thus, the Bible has long been recognized as one book, even though it actually contains sixty-six smaller books ranging in size from one page (such as 2 John and 3 John) to 150 chapters (such as Psalms).

The Bible is divided into two parts, the Old Testament and the New Testament. This is not an arbitrary division. "Testament" means "covenant" or "sacred agreement," and the Bible is divided into two basic agreements between God and humanity. Jews regard the Old Testament as God's word to His people. Christians added the New Testament after the coming of Jesus. It reveals the new covenant between God and His people that Christians believe transcends the old covenant.

What are these agreements? The old covenant tradition-ally refers to the Law of Moses found in the first five books of the Old Testament. The law was God's way of governing Israel. In fact, Jews classified 613 laws in the Old Testament that God's people were bound to keep. These laws, however, aren't all there is to the Old Testament. There are also the teachings of the prophets, the spiritual poetry of Psalms, the moral tales of Jonah, Ruth and others. The Old Testament shows us people who are human, just like us. These people, like David and Solomon, are full of flaws and constantly fail, but through their faith in God's abiding power, even they rise to greatness.

The new covenant found in the New Testament refers to God's new relationship with His people through grace. Its message is simple. In it Jesus says, "Come to Me all who are weary and heavy-laden and I will give you rest." The New Testament brought new joy, hope, and love into the lives of the people.

Today, Jews and Christians consider the Bible an essential teaching tool and guide for living. While Jews use only the Old Testament, Christians use both Old and New Testaments.

But this is just the beginning. Historians use it as a research tool and scholars study it in the original languages. Archaeologists employ it in their search for ancient villages and cities. Muslims study it because they believe that they, like Jews, are descended from Abraham. But for all there is enlightenment, instruction, insight, and hope.

BOOKS OF THE BIBLE AND THEIR ABBREVIATIONS—KING JAMES VERSION

OLD TESTAMENT

Genesis–*Gen.*
Exodus–*Exod.*
Leviticus–*Lev.*
Numbers–*Num.*
Deuteronomy–*Deut.*
Joshua–*Josh.*
Judges–*Judg.*
Ruth–*Ruth*
1 Samuel–*1 Sam.*
2 Samuel–*2 Sam.*
1 Kings–*1 Kings*
2 Kings–*2 Kings*
1 Chronicles–*1 Chron.*
2 Chronicles–*2 Chron.*
Ezra–*Ezra*
Nehemiah–*Neh.*
Esther–*Esther*
Job–*Job*
Psalms–*Ps. (pl. Pss.)*
Proverbs–*Prov.*

Ecclesiastes–*Eccles.*
Song of Solomon–*Song of Sol.*
Isaiah–*Isa.*
Jeremiah–*Jer.*
Lamentations–*Lam.*
Ezekiel–*Ezek.*
Daniel–*Dan.*
Hosea–*Hos.*
Joel–*Joel*
Amos–*Amos*
Obadiah–*Obad.*
Jonah–*Jon.*
Micah–*Mic.*
Nahum–*Nah.*
Habakkuk–*Hab.*
Zephaniah–*Zeph.*
Haggai–*Hag.*
Zechariah–*Zech.*
Malachi–*Mal.*

NEW TESTAMENT

Matthew–*Matt.*
Mark–*Mark*
Luke–*Luke*
John–*John*
Acts of the Apostles–
  Acts
Romans–*Rom.*
1 Corinthians–*1 Cor.*
2 Corinthians–*2 Cor.*
Galatians–*Gal.*
Ephesians–*Eph.*
Philippians–*Phil.*
Colossians–*Col.*
1 Thessalonians–
  1 Thess.

2 Thessalonians–
  2 Thess.
1 Timothy–*1 Tim.*
2 Timothy–*2 Tim.*
Titus–*Titus*
Philemon–*Philem.*
Hebrews–*Heb.*
James–*James*
1 Peter–*1 Pet.*
2 Peter–*2 Pet.*
1 John–*1 John*
2 John–*2 John*
3 John–*3 John*
Jude–*Jude*
Revelation–*Rev.*

CHAPTER ONE

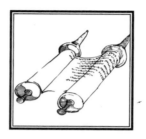

WHAT IS IN THE BIBLE?

WHAT CAN WE READ IN THE BIBLE?

The Bible is composed of sixty-six separate books. There are thirty-nine books in the Old Testament, twenty-seven in the New Testament. These books include many different styles and forms of writing. For instance, the first five books of the Old Testament are Moses' books of the law. They include many laws and much history. There are also books entirely comprised of history such as Joshua and Esther; poetry such as Job and the Song of Solomon; and prophecy such as Isaiah and Malachi.

The New Testament contains history including Matthew and Acts; letters or epistles to the church from Paul and others found in Romans and Jude, and more prophecy to be discovered in Revelation.

Strangely enough, the Bible contains forms of writing we might not expect. It includes drama in Job and Song of Solomon; parables or short stories that teach a point in the Gospels—Matthew, Mark, Luke, and John; sermons in Deuteronomy and the Gospels; and poetry in Psalms and Isaiah.

WHAT PERIODS OF HISTORY ARE COVERED IN THE BIBLE?

The Old Testament starts at the beginning of creation when God made heaven and earth, the plants and animals, and Adam and Eve. It moves through history to the time of Malachi, the last prophet, who wrote around 450-400 B.C. The Old Testament touches on many different times in human history, including the rise and fall of the Tower of Babel, and the ascendancy of Assyria, Babylon, Greece, and Rome. And it tells many marvelous stories of the lives of saints who lived outside of Israel—Ruth, Esther, Job.

However, the real purpose of the Old Testament was to tell Jewish history—the rises, falls, trials, and tribulations of the Jewish people. This story starts at the beginning of Jewish history with the life of Abraham and continues to the last rulers of Judah (the second Jewish nation after it split into Israel and Judah) before the people were taken into slavery by Babylon. It follows that period with the history of the rebuilding of the Jewish Temple in Jerusalem—Ezra—

through the rebuilding of the walls of Jerusalem—Nehemiah. The Old Testament ends in approximately 400 B.C. with the prophecy of Malachi, who told the people to await the coming of the Messiah.

The New Testament starts near A.D. 49 with the book Galatians. The New Testament primarily covers the life of Jesus, in the Gospels, and the founding of the early Christian church, in Acts. The last book, Revelation, was probably written just before the turn of the second century in A.D. 95. Many scholars believe this book describes a future time of struggle and the eventual second coming of Jesus Christ.

WHAT IS IN THE OLD TESTAMENT?

The section of the modern Bible we call the Old Testament is a series of thirty-nine separate books or writings considered sacred by both Jews and Christians. It begins with a history of the world from the Creation, then narrows in scope to tell the history of the Hebrew people, including their trials, triumphs, and tragedies, and their laws, successes, and failures under God's rule. The Old Testament includes history, poetry, drama, parables, prophecy, sermons, and numerous other literary forms. It is far and away the most important historical book from before the time of Christ, and scholars, archaeologists, teachers, professors, politicians, and others rely on it as a source of material for everything from speeches to important clues about where to search for a new archaeological site.

WHERE DID THE BOOKS OF THE OLD TESTAMENT COME FROM?

To ask the source of the Old Testament is to ask what is the source of inspiration of the Holy Spirit. As noted, some writers of the Old Testament were historians. They collected, repeated, and interpreted what they learned from the oral and written traditions. Other books, like Job and the Song of Solomon, were dramas. Deuteronomy is in the form of a compilation of Moses' last sermons to the Israelite people just before they entered the land of Canaan. The books of Obadiah, Nahum, Isaiah, and others were prophecies inspired by God and written by the prophet or his followers. Many Jews and Christians today believe that Scripture, while written by the hands of men, is the word of God, passed on from generation to generation.

HOW MANY BOOKS ARE IN THE OLD TESTAMENT?

In modern Protestant translations of the Old Testament, there are thirty-nine books. There are twenty-four books in the Hebrew writings. Along with a different organization of the historical books, the Protestant translations count the

writings of the Minor Prophets as individual books, while
the Hebrew Scripture counts them as a single book.

The thirty-nine books are:

The Law of Moses (also, the Torah, or Pentateuch):

Genesis
Exodus
Leviticus
Numbers
Deuteronomy

The Historical Books:

Joshua
Judges
Ruth
1 and 2 Samuel
1 and 2 Kings
1 and 2 Chronicles
Ezra
Nehemiah
Esther

The Books of Poetry:

Job
Psalms
Proverbs
Ecclesiastes
Song of Solomon
The Major Prophets:
Isaiah
Jeremiah and Lamentations
Ezekiel
Daniel
Hosea

The Minor Prophets:
>Joel
>
>Amos
>
>Obadiah
>
>Jonah
>
>Micah
>
>Nahum
>
>Habakkuk
>
>Zephaniah
>
>Haggai
>
>Zechariah
>
>Malachi

WHO DECIDED WHICH BOOKS TO INCLUDE IN THE OLD TESTAMENT?

The history of how the thirty-nine books of the Old Testament came to be included as the word of God is fascinating and poignant. During the period from Moses to the time of Christ, these books and others were collected and classified. Many rabbis argued about the authority of some books—Esther, because in that book there is no mention of God; Proverbs, because of certain apparent contradictions; Ecclesiastes, because the author seemed to have no faith—but it wasn't until the time of Christ that the present collection became "canon." To talk about the canon of scripture is to speak of a collection of books that conform to a standard of doctrine, faith, and integrity.

Some books had been questioned. Some scholars believe that these disputes were settled in A.D. 90, at the Jewish Council of Jamnia. The arguments were all laid out by the rabbis, and in the end Esther, Ecclesiastes, Proverbs, and the Song of Solomon were summarily accepted.

How do scholars know if an ancient book is the Word of God and worthy of inclusion in the Bible? There are several criteria scholars have used throughout history. First: was the book inspired by the Holy Spirit? That is, was it recognized from the very beginning that these words had the immortal and supernatural stamp of God's life? Second: was the writer a prophet? Third: was the book accepted as authoritative from the beginning and throughout history—had the hallowed rabbis and leaders of the church hailed the text as God's word and written to that effect?

These three tests were always imposed, and throughout history both the Jewish leaders and the consensus among the early Christian leaders have agreed that these thirty-nine books are the very word of God.

What of the Apocrypha? Seven of these books were received as canon by the Roman Catholic Church at the Council of Trent in A.D. 1545. But none of the Jewish or Protestant groups have received these seven (or the other eight) and they are regarded as man-made literature.

WERE ANY BOOKS EXCLUDED?
During the 400-year period between the end of the writings of the Old Testament and the beginning of the writings

of the New Testament, the fifteen books we now call "The Apocrypha" were written. "Apocrypha" means "hidden." Neither Jews nor Protestants consider the Apocrypha the direct word of God. However, Roman Catholics accept twelve of the books as part of God's revelation to mankind.

Like the Old Testament, the Apocrypha contains books of history, like 1 and 2 Maccabees, as well as fantastic stories with wild images like Bel and the Dragon. These fifteen books were not included in the Old Testament canon for various reasons: some were considered inaccurate, some were fantastical, some were written by people who were not considered prophets.

The Apocrypha in the Catholic canon are Tobit, Judith, Wisdom of Solomon, Ecclesiasticus, Baruch, 1 and 2 Maccabees, Epistle to Jeremiah, the Prayer of Azariah and the Song of the Three Young Men, Susanna, the addition to Esther, and Bel and the Dragon. Martin Luther considered these stories helpful, but not the word of God. In the Apocrypha we have stories such as that of Tobias, the son of Tobit. With the angel Raphael in mortal form, Tobias performed two miracles: he rid Sarah, his own betrothed, of a demon; and he healed Tobit of blindness. In another story, that of Susanna, the young woman is accused of adultery but Daniel proves her true by finding inconsistencies in the stories of her accusers.

The three books of the Apocrypha that Catholics do not consider canon are 1 and 2 Esdras and the Prayer of Manasseh.

There are also a series of books called the pseudepigrapha, a Greek term meaning "false writings." Religious leaders felt that these books, written in Hebrew, Greek, or

Aramaic between 200 B.C. and A.D. 100, were not written by prophets, nor did their writings have the stamp of the Spirit either in factual information or divine anointing. Thus, they were never considered to be the word of God. Some of the better-known of these ancient writings are:

The Life of Adam and Eve
Enoch
The Book of Jubilees
The Lives of the Prophets
3 and 4 Maccabees
The Assumption of Moses
Psalm 151

WHY ARE THE BOOKS OF THE OLD TESTAMENT IN THEIR PRESENT ORDER?

Throughout history, we find many writings that refer to the thirty-nine books in various chronological, spiritual, or memorable orders. The books were generally referred to as the law, the prophets, and the writings. In A.D. 400, the Jewish Talmud referred to the books in the same order in which we find them today in the Hebrew Bible.

However, the Christian Bible is different. In A.D. 170, a church father named Melito of Sardis traveled to Palestine with the express purpose of determining the canon of the Old Testament. He came up with the thirty-nine books in roughly the same order we have them today in the English Bible. Other church fathers, in referring to the Old

Testament, would list the books in various orders, but eventually, when Gutenberg printed the first Bibles in Mainz, Germany, in 1455, the order was formalized as the standard for all succeeding Bibles.

Jews also devised a system of chapters and verses different than the one used in modern Protestant Bibles today. Stephen Langdon, Archbishop of Canterbury, divided the Old Testament into its present chapter and verse form during his lifetime. He died in A.D. 1228.

HOW IS THE SONG OF SOLOMON DIFFERENT FROM OTHER BOOKS IN THE OLD TESTAMENT?

Unlike other books in the Old Testament, this book does not mention God's name. The words, taken by themselves, are a poetic tribute to love. They form some of the most touching, intimate, and evocative writing in the Bible. But why is this book included in the Bible? Many scholars interpret these writings to be an allegory, a story about God's love for His Chosen people.

WHAT DOES THE BOOK OF PSALMS OFFER US?

Psalms offers comfort, repose, and spiritual inspiration. This Scripture offers solace in moments of grief or loss, or it can inspire the reader to lofty heights of pure joy. The moving words in Psalms soon had a special place in the liturgy of the Jews, and in the Temple in Jerusalem, choirs would sing psalms to the accompaniment of musical instruments.

Many of the Psalms are attributed to David, who would have written them in the years around 1000 B.C. Others are thought to have been written in later years—some as late as 200 B.C. But no matter how the Psalms came to us, God's voice and inspiration can be felt in their words.

HOW MANY VERSES ARE IN THE OLD TESTAMENT?

It depends on which Old Testament version you're using. However, the King James Version was completely dissected and tabulated by Dr. Thomas Hartwell Horne. He was born in London, England, in 1780 and, after being educated at Christ's Hospital School, he became a lawyer's clerk. He published his first book at the age of twenty and went on to write many others. But his *summa bonum* was *Introduction to the Study of the Scriptures* which included a number of statistics about the King James Version of the Bible. They are:

Old Testament
    Books–39
    Chapters–929
    Verses–23,214
    Words–593,493
    Letters–2,728,100

Middle verse of entire Bible–Psalm 118:8
Longest verse of the Bible–Esther 9:8
Shortest verse of the Bible–John 11:35 ("Jesus wept.")
Longest chapter–Psalm 119
Shortest chapter–Psalm 1171

WHAT IS IN THE NEW TESTAMENT?

The New Testament includes twenty-seven books and writings by the disciples, "learners," and apostles, or "sent ones," of Jesus Christ. These books are accepted by the Christian church worldwide as the final word of God to the world before Jesus returns to begin His eternal kingdom. It is "New" in contrast to the Old Testament of the Jews, and it is a "Testament" in that it represents God's final covenant or agreement with mankind. It is considered the unique, eternal and supernatural revelation of God through His spirit to all who listen. The New Testament is divided into four parts:

Gospels ("Good News")
Matthew
Mark
Luke
John

History
Acts

Epistles
Romans
1 and 2 Corinthians
Galatians
Ephesians
Philippians
Colossians
1 and 2 Thessalonians
1 and 2 Timothy
Titus
Philemon
Hebrews
James
1 and 2 Peter
1, 2, and 3 John
Jude

Prophecy
Revelation

WHEN DID THE NEW TESTAMENT BEGIN?

The Old Testament concludes with the prophecy of Malachi, written about 400 B.C. The New Testament began with the letter of James, about A.D. 48-50, followed by Galatians, written anywhere from A.D. 49-55. Other letters followed: 1 and 2 Thessalonians (A.D. 51), 1 and 2 Corinthians (A.D. 56-57), and Romans (A.D. 58). The first

Gospel was probably Mark, (perhaps A.D. 50-60), followed by Luke (possibly around A.D. 60).

WERE ANY BOOKS EXCLUDED?

A number of different books were in circulation during the second and third centuries when church leaders were discussing what books should be included in the New Testament. Some of these books were by church fathers, including Clement of Rome, whose epistles to the Corinthians, Clement 1 and 2, were considered by some to be worthy of inclusion in the New Testament. These books were finally rejected because the writer, Clement, had not been an eyewitness to Christ.

A number of other writings existed, grouped under the titles of church fathers. The better-known ones include the letters of Ignatius to the Ephesians, Romans, and Philadelphians, the Epistle of Polycarp to the Philippians, the Martyrdom of Polycarp, the Didache, the Epistle of Barnabas, the Shepherd of Hermas, the Epistle of Diognetus, and the Fragment of Papias. All these worthy documents were rejected as the very word of God for various reasons, but primarily because they were not eyewitness accounts of the life of Christ.

Other books are known as the New Testament Apocrypha and include the Gospel of Thomas, the Gospel of Mary, and others. These were written in many cases by unknown writers who claimed the name of someone close to Jesus to gain authority. However, these books were always regarded as "non-canonical"—not part of the canon of scripture—and thus were not included in the New Testament.

WHO DECIDED WHAT THE NEW TESTAMENT WOULD INCLUDE?

Throughout the ages, various people have argued for and against the inclusion of certain books in the New Testament. At one time or another, it's fair to assume that every book has been criticized by someone.

In the early church, the fathers—Ignatius, Clement, Polycarp—all recognized certain books as canonical. By A.D. 140, an early heretic named Marcion had accepted an edited Gospel of Luke and ten epistles of Paul as authoritative. He rejected the entire Old Testament, saying that it did not speak of the same God as the New Testament. As a result, the church fathers had to determine whether other epistles were canonical—like James and 1 and 2 Peter—as well as the other Gospels by Matthew, Mark, and John.

Responding to Marcion, various church fathers recognized four Gospels, Acts, all thirteen Epistles of Paul, all the other epistles (James, Peter, John, Jude), and Revelation. In A.D. 367 Athanasius of Alexandria issued a list of both Old Testament and New Testament documents that composed the canon. This list was repeated by Jerome and Augustine in the western branch of the church. It comprises our present order and was later repeated in many of the codexes that came to collect all twenty-seven of the New Testament books.

The first New Testament text to appear with chapters and

verses was a Greek edition published by a Paris printer named Robert Stephens in 1551. In 1555 he brought out an edition of the Vulgate which uses our present chapter and verse system.

HOW MANY VERSES ARE THERE IN THE NEW TESTAMENT?

According to the statistics gathered by Thomas Hartwell Horne[2], the King James Version breaks down as follows:

New Testament
- Books–27
- Chapters–260
- Verses–7,959
- Words–181,253
- Letters–838,380

WHAT IS IN THE BOOK OF REVELATION?

Revelation, the last book of the New Testament, is a form of prophetic writing that highlights the second coming of Jesus and the final judgement and all it entails. Revelation says that in the end God will right every wrong, bring to justice all those who defy Him, and give peace to His beloved. He will create a new heaven and earth in which His kingdom of goodness, peace, justice, and truth will never end.

The style of writing, using literary symbols, imagery, and cataclysmic actions over the grand sweep of heaven, earth, and hell is called apocalyptic. Much of this scripture is written in this form to mask from enemies its primary purpose of encouraging early Christians to resist pagan rule and influence.

WHAT ARE THE DEAD SEA SCROLLS?

An Arabic Bedouin, searching for his sheep among caves near the Dead Sea, made one of the greatest archaeological finds of modern history. These caves were located in the sandy cliffs about a mile west of the northwestern corner of the Dead Sea, near a town known as Qumran.

So far, eleven caves have been discovered in which various scrolls were buried in large, clay-fired jars. One cave, number four, has yielded fragments from some 382 manuscripts of which 100 are Old Testament documents.

One of the more magnificent finds is a complete scroll of Isaiah. There is also a commentary on Habakkuk that includes a complete copy of Habakkuk 1 and 2 in its text.

The people of Qumran lived there between 140 B.C. and A.D. 67. Most scholars believe these people were Essenes, members of a small sect of Judaism who wished to remove themselves from the evils of urban life. They were ascetics, devoted to the study of the Old Testament. There are no New Testament documents found among the hidden scrolls, mainly because the first New Testament epistles were penned after Qumran had been destroyed. However, there is much debate about whether John the Baptist or even Jesus had dealings with the sect. There is no proof of either, but many scholars still search for a connection.

The Dead Sea Scrolls have provided invaluable information about how we got our Bible. Up to their discovery, we knew the text of the Old Testament largely as a result of the scribesmanship and copying abilities of a group known as the Masoretes. These scholars transcribed the Old Testament from about A.D. 400 to the time of the printing press. The oldest documents we have from the Masoretes are from about A.D. 900.

With the Dead Sea Scrolls, though, a jump back of nearly a thousand years is possible. At least fragments of every one of the Old Testament books are found among the Dead Sea Scrolls, except for the book of Esther. Thus, these scrolls provide a powerful affirmation and insight into the original sources of the Old Testament to scholars the world over.

Moreover, many other scrolls found at Qumran tell much about the everyday life and religious thought of the period from about 140 years before the birth of Jesus and possibly even during the time He lived. From them we have come to know a lot about the Essenes, their beliefs and commitments, how they lived and died, and what Jewish life was like outside their community. Though some scholars have tried to show a connection between Jesus and Qumran, no definitive link has been established. However, the Dead Sea Scrolls illuminate our understanding of such subjects as Jewish Gnosticism, a mystical system of beliefs that Paul wrote against in Colossians. They are a providential find that has increased our understanding and reverence for the Bible.

CAN BOOKS BE ADDED TO THE BIBLE?

Since the early church, the Bible canon or standard has been considered final. Though some scholars have questioned whether some books should be included in the Bible, few have questioned whether any of the other ancient writings should be added. Paul said in 1 Corinthians that "whether there be prophecies, they shall fail" (1 Cor. 13:8). Some interpret this to mean that the ability to speak the word of God without error ended with the apostles.

Also, in the book of Revelation, the last book of the New Testament, the author offers this stern rejoinder: "I testify unto every man that heareth the words of the prophecy of this book: if any man shall add unto these things, God shall add unto him the plagues that are written in this book: and if any man shall take away from the words of the book of this prophecy, God shall take away his part out of the book of life, and out of the holy city, and from the things which are written in this book" (Rev. 22:18-19).

Thus, many conservative scholars believe that God has finished revealing His word to His people and that there are no more instructions, laws, reminders, or prophecies that we need to know.

HAS THE BIBLE CHANGED FOR THE MODERN READER?

The King James Version remains one of the most poetic of the English language translations. It has been followed by many contemporary English language Bibles. Some of these include the Revised Standard Version (RSV), 1952; the American Standard Version (ASV), 1901; The Jerusalem Bible (TJB), 1966; The New American Standard Bible (NASB), 1971; The Living Bible (TLB), 1972; The New International Version (NIV), 1985; and The Revised English Bible, 1989. These versions represent everything from highly literal but formal English (as in the NASB) to the loose, subjective paraphrases of The Living Bible.

A multitude of Bibles for every taste can be found in Christian bookstores today. Many of these are study Bibles, arranged with notes and thoughts for seemingly every possible problem or need. There are Bibles for children, middle-grade readers, teenagers, single adults, college students, career men and women, husbands, wives, families, retired people, church leaders, pastors, and even dysfunctional, recovering, or fast-paced folks.

CHAPTER TWO

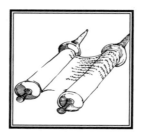

WHO WROTE THE BIBLE?

WHO WROTE THE
OLD TESTAMENT?

Many books of the Old Testament were written by the people whose names they bear—such as Isaiah, Jeremiah, and Ezekiel. In other books, the author is not named, like Jonah and 1 and 2 Samuel, but the identity of the authors has been passed down through time. For some books, we don't have positive knowledge of who wrote them—like Ruth and Esther—but we can speculate on the basis of various biblical clues such as the people who are referred to, the way the story is written, stylistic points, and other means.

Many of the earliest stories were probably passed down by oral tradition. At some point, though, someone gathered the complete oral tradition and recorded it in a book. Writers like Moses and Samuel would be, in that sense, compilers as well as writers.

Many people of faith believe that Moses, who possibly lived about 1520 B.C. to 1400 B.C., wrote the first five books of the Old Testament, sometimes called the "Law," or "Torah" in Hebrew. The five books are also called the "Pentateuch," which means "five books" in Greek.

Moses probably wrote on papyrus leaves, a kind of paper made from papyrus stalks. Papyrus is a reed that grows in marshy areas, on the banks of rivers, and in shallow waters on rivers' edges in the lands of the Middle East. People cut the stalks and lined them up next to one another to make half a page. Then they took other stalks and lined them up perpendicularly to the first group. They pressed and glued the stalks together to form a page. Papyrus paper was rough, brittle, and didn't last long, and many people preferred to write on clay tablets. But papyrus could hold more writing and was more portable, and it came to be preferred. Papyrus was used in Egypt from about 2000 B.C.

It's possible that Moses wrote on papyrus leaves that were then fashioned into a scroll. This was accomplished by gluing together flat leaves of papyrus about a foot square, and then rolling them up in a long coil. A book the length of Genesis might have been sixty feet long when laid out end to end. Picture him sitting cross-legged in his tent, dipping a sharp reed into ink made of crushed charcoal and water. He would have used an early alphabet, or perhaps a combination of letters from other cultures—Akkadian, Ugaritic, Sinaitic—or perhaps a precursor of the twenty-two letter Hebrew alphabet. We know that such writing was common back then. On the walls of the Egyptian turquoise mines at Serabit-el Khadim can be found the writings of Semitic miners, apparently prayers.

Thus, Moses puts pen to paper to record the great events that made up the history of the Jewish people. It's probable that Moses learned the history of the Jews that he related in Genesis by hearing stories that had been passed down through generations of Jews. This is "oral tradition." It's the primary way that stories are passed from one generation to the next. We still do this at family gatherings, telling and retelling the stories of our family history. Moses may have been writing what he heard around the campfire, on the road, and in the palace, or what he learned from reading other "books."

It's also possible that Moses learned Hebrew history during his forty years in the court of Egypt. He sat at his mother's knee in the early years when she was his nurse in the court and he later had access to the Egyptian libraries. We know from Acts 7 that Moses was a "learned man."

On the other hand, God may simply have revealed the stories to Moses. Throughout Hebrew history, prophets claimed to have received direct revelation from God through visions, angelic visitations, dreams, personal meditation, and other means. It's possible that Moses was personally instructed by God in all that he wrote down.

However it came about, archaeologists have confirmed that the Old Testament is often accurate in its use of names, places, peoples, and times. Even though the first ancient writings have long perished, we have copies that have been passed on by godly people who considered them the very word of God. As a result, each book was transcribed with care.

IN WHAT LANGUAGE WAS THE OLD TESTAMENT WRITTEN?

Most of the Old Testament was written in Hebrew. But some books, such as Daniel and Ezra, contain passages in Aramaic, which was the Assyrian language of diplomacy during the centuries before the third century when Alexander the Great's conquests made Greek the international language of the world.

WHO WROTE THE NEW TESTAMENT?

Many conservative Christian scholars attribute the writing of the books to specific known people.

Matthew, the tax collector, wrote Matthew.

John Mark wrote the book of Mark, presumably with the help of Peter.

Luke was not a disciple, but a Greek physician. He wrote the books of Luke and Acts.

John, the son of Zebedee and brother of James, wrote John; 1, 2, and 3 John; and Revelation.

Paul wrote the next 13 epistles. He was not one of the twelve original disciples but was called later by Jesus on the Damascus road.

No one is sure who wrote Hebrews.

James, the brother of Jesus, wrote James. He was not a disciple but became a follower of Jesus' teachings after Jesus' death.

Peter wrote 1 and 2 Peter.

Jude, the brother of Jesus and James, wrote Jude. He also was not a disciple but became a believer after Jesus' death and resurrection.

The New Testament is a collection of writings by individuals who were describing their own experiences and perceptions. For instance, most of Paul's epistles were written to churches, which were named by city or region, for example, Romans for Rome and Corinthians for Corinth. Paul also wrote letters to individuals—Timothy, Titus, Philemon, an elder named Gaius (3 John). Several books were written to reach specific audiences—Hebrews for certain Jews, Luke for someone named Theophilus, which means "friend of God" and thus might refer to anyone who is a believer, and Mark for people of Roman descent. Matthew was probably written for Jews, John for Greeks. Some epistles were for everyone in general—James, 1 John, and Jude.

The churches and individuals who received these books and letters preserved them, copied them, and passed them to others. These individual writings circulated throughout the Roman world until the last decade of the first century, when some books began to appear in collections. By the second century there was a collection of 13 epistles of Paul. Early Christians also chose four "gospels," and eventually all the books of the New Testament were brought together and recognized by various councils and leaders of the churches as the definitive collection of the word of God—the New Testament.

Scholars, scribes, and others who regarded the books as sacred copied and passed on the collected books. We have a fragment of a passage of the Book of John from about A.D. 125 (we know that it is a copy from the lettering), so it's clear that people were making copies at that time. Christians already considered these books to be sacred, and indeed the authors in many cases indicate clearly that the writings should be circulated. It was only a matter of time before many copies were available throughout the Roman Empire. In A.D. 95, Clement of Rome was secretary of his church and wrote a letter to the church in Corinth that quotes freely from Romans, 1 and 2 Corinthians, and other letters. Clearly, he had a collection on hand.

IN WHAT LANGUAGE WAS THE NEW TESTAMENT WRITTEN?

The New Testament is all written in Koine (pronounced "coin-ay") Greek. This was the common Greek of the times, used by average people and by diplomats. It's a "lower" form of Greek, different from the "classical" Greek used by authors like Homer, Plato, and Aristotle. Koine Greek was the perfect language for the New Testament because many people the world over spoke and read it. This made evangelism and the spread of Christianity much easier.

It's also possible that some books such as Matthew were written originally in Aramaic, the common language of the Jews and the language that Jesus probably spoke.

WHO FIRST TRANSLATED THE BIBLE?

Greek translations of the Hebrew Bible already existed by the time of Jesus. The Septuagint was especially important.

Jerome's Vulgate, a Latin translation completed in A.D. 405, became the standard Bible for many years since Latin was the common language of the educated classes in the world at that time. Jerome worked directly from the Hebrew and Greek texts, as well as from earlier Latin efforts, while living in a cave in Bethlehem next to the Grotto of the Nativity, then believed to be the birthplace of Jesus.

WHEN WAS THE BIBLE TRANSLATED INTO ENGLISH?

The Bible has been translated from its original languages into many English versions. Parts of the Bible were translated into Old English (Anglo-Saxon) in the late tenth century. A very important English-language Bible translation was an illustrated version by John Wycliffe, an Englishman. The Wycliffe translation of the New Testament came out in 1380 and the Old Testament arrived two years later. Wycliffe had several scholars helping him with the translation, which was based on the Latin Vulgate, not the original languages of Hebrew, Aramaic, and Greek. All the copies were written by hand. Only 170 copies are known to exist today.

Other versions in English followed, notably that of William Tyndale. From the time of his early training (he was born in 1494), he wanted to create a translation of the New Testament that would reach the common people of England. He labored away, but the Roman Catholic church opposed him. He left England to search for printers in Europe, finally settling on a printer in Worms, Germany. This printer brought out an English language translation of the New Testament in 1525. The printer finished 3,000 copies, and soon smuggled copies began to reach England. The Tyndale version proved to be successful and readable. By 1534, England's King Henry VIII formed the Church of England when he broke with the Roman Catholic Church. However, Tyndale, who was hiding in Antwerp, was betrayed by an English Roman Catholic in 1536. He was tried, condemned to death as a heretic, strangled, and his body was burned at the stake. Although Tyndale's translations were banned and burned in England, he had awakened the king to the need for an English version of the Bible for the common people, and this was his lasting legacy.

Other English translations followed Tyndale's: those of Miles Coverdale in 1535, Thomas Matthew in 1537, and the "Great Bible" in 1539, so-called because of its great size and sumptuous illustrations. The Geneva Bible came later, in 1557, and was the first to incorporate chapters and verses. A revision of that Bible, called the "Bishop's Bible," appeared in 1568 during the reign of Queen Elizabeth I.

The Roman Catholic Church created its own version to compete with the many Protestant translations; the Rheims-Douai Bible was completed in 1610. Unfortunately, it was translated from the Latin Vulgate, not the original languages.

The premiere English translation of centuries ago remains the King James Version. In 1607, King James I of England, successor to Queen Elizabeth I, ordered a new English translation of the Bible. He wanted to leave his mark on history with an excellent, literary translation of the entire Bible. To this end he commissioned forty-seven of the best Greek and Hebrew scholars in England. They were divided into six teams, three for the Old Testament, two for the New Testament, and one for the Apocrypha. The King James Version was finished just two years and nine months after it was begun and was printed in 1611. It was an immediate sensation, owing to its beautiful and poetic use of English as well as its integrity and accuracy.

INTO HOW MANY LANGUAGES HAS THE BIBLE BEEN TRANSLATED?

Parts of the Bible are now available in more than 2,070 languages. Frequently, in translating the Bible, missionaries have created alphabets for the languages and peoples they've served, bringing to them for the first time not only God's word, but the written word. Usually, new translators start with one of the gospels, John being the easiest in the original Greek. From there they proceed to other books. Bible translation into new languages requires a lifetime of commitment and service for the translators.

WHAT ARE
ILLUMINATED BIBLES?

During the Middle Ages before the advent of the printing press, the Bible was copied by hand by monks living in monasteries. Sometimes these monks "illuminated" their copies with drawings. They were especially skilled at illustrating the first letter of a chapter or book with coils, graphics, elaborate designs, miniature pictures, and other forms. Sometimes these were done in real silver or gold which seemed to glow, hence the name "illuminated." These Bibles were written on fine white vellum paper—the scraped and preserved skin of a calf or lamb. They were expensive to produce and own. It was with reverence and joy that a person of the nobility in the Middle Ages opened the text and read to their little ones about the great people and events of their faith.

It took illustrators many years to complete the illuminated text of a single book, and sometimes a lifetime. After the printing press came along, few illuminated Bibles were produced.

WHO PRODUCED THE FIRST
PRINTED BIBLE?

Johannes Gutenberg, using movable type, printed the first Bible in A.D. 1455, in Mainz, Germany. The text was written in Latin. Gutenberg arranged it in three volumes that were lavishly illustrated with designs and pictures on the first pages of each new book. No one knows how many copies were originally made. There were no chapter or verse divisions in the Gutenberg version. Gutenberg printed his Bibles on costly vellum. Few could afford such a Bible except those in high places in the church and royalty. Sometimes, these books were commissioned by a king or governor as gifts for his nobles.

Today, there are only about forty known copies of Gutenberg's Bible, housed in various places including the Library of Congress in Washington, D.C., and the British Library in London, England.

HOW MANY COPIES OF THE BIBLE HAVE BEEN PRINTED?

There is no way to accurately calculate the number of Bibles that have been produced the world over. There are innumerable organizations, Bible societies and other groups that publish Bibles in a multitude of languages. Eighty percent of the world's peoples have access to the Bible in their language.

The International Bible Society (IBS) reports that in 1994 there were 58,686,000 complete Bibles produced. In the United States, each household averages four; that's more than a billion.

WHY ARE BIBLES FOUND IN HOTEL AND MOTEL ROOMS?

Most of these Bibles are donated to hotels and motels by the Gideons. The Gideons began in 1898 when two businessmen, John Nicholson and Samuel Hill, met in the Central Hotel in Boscobel, Wisconsin. They discovered their mutual faith in Christ and spent time together reading the Bible and praying. A year later, with W. J. Knight, they met again and formed an organization for traveling men that they called "The Gideons," after the name of the Old Testament judge who defeated 120,000 Midianites with 300 men. In 1908, the organization began placing Bibles and New Testament texts in public places like hotel rooms. They also gave Bibles to school children, nurses, soldiers, prisoners, and others. They are dedicated to spreading the news of the Gospel to travelers and to those who are alone.

United States membership for the Gideons has climbed to 76,600 men, with international members numbering more than 100,000. Since they began, the Gideons have distributed more than thirty-seven million Bibles, and 630 million copies of the New Testament.

CHAPTER THREE

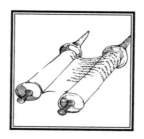

WHAT DOES THE BIBLE TEACH US?

WHAT IS SCRIPTURE?

The word "Scripture" comes to us from the Late Latin word *scriptus* and the Middle English word *scriptura,* and means "writing." Scripture generally refers to the sacred writings of the Bible. Frequently, the Old and New Testaments use the word Scripture to denote any specific text, paragraph, verse, or even a few words.

WHAT DOES THE BIBLE TELL US ABOUT SIN?

The Greek word for sin, *hamartia,* means "to miss the mark," as in a fired arrow missing a bull's-eye. Romans 3:23 says this about sin: "All have sinned, and come short of the glory of God."

One biblical definition of sin is that mankind was thrust into a state of "original sin" in which man's nature was corrupted and tainted, through the disobedience of Adam and Eve in the Garden. God gave them a special test—not to eat of the fruit of the tree of knowledge of good and evil. If they were to eat of that fruit, they would die. They would die spiritually—that is, their inner spirit would be separated from the life of God. They would no longer be able to experience the full joy, love, and peace of divinity. Secondly, they would die physically—their spirits would be separated from their bodies and their bodies would become inert, unanimated, ready to be buried. Finally, they would die eternally—separated from God forever in hell.

How will we pay for our sins? The New Testament says that we can't pay for them on our own. But God made a way for them to be paid—by Jesus' death on the cross. God has promised that if we put our faith in Him, we will be forgiven, "born again," and set free from the penalty of sin forever.

WHY DID GOD GIVE US THE TEN COMMANDMENTS?

The Ten Commandments are the basic principles of civilized human behavior that God gave to His chosen people through Moses. They are revealed to God's people in the Old Testament, both in Exodus 20 and in Deuteronomy 6. These are not laws governed by secular authorities, but God's plan for civilized living. They are as follows:

1) Thou shalt have no other gods before me.

2) Thou shalt not make unto thee any graven image, or any likeness of any thing that is in heaven above, or that is in the earth beneath, or that is in the water under the earth.

Thou shalt not bow down thyself to them, nor serve them: for I am a jealous God, visiting the iniquity of the fathers upon the children unto the third and fourth generation of them that hate me;

And shewing mercy unto thousands of them that love me, and keep my commandments.

3) Thou shalt not take the name of the Lord thy God in vain; for the Lord will not hold him guiltless that taketh His name in vain.

4) Remember the sabbath day, keep it holy.

Six days shalt thou labour, and do all thy work:

But the seventh day is the sabbath of the Lord thy God: in it thou shalt not do any work, thou, nor thy son, nor thy daughter, nor thy maidservant, nor thy cattle, nor thy stranger that is within thy gates.

5) Honour thy father and thy mother: that thy days may be long upon the land which the Lord thy God giveth thee.

6) Thou shalt not kill.

7) Thou shalt not commit adultery.

8) Thou shalt not steal.

9) Thou shalt not bear false witness against thy neighbor.

10) Thou shalt not covet thy neighbor's house, thou shalt not covet thy neighbor's wife, nor his manservant, nor his maidservant, nor his ox, nor his ass, nor any thing that is thy neighbor's.

DOES THE BIBLE DESCRIBE HEAVEN?

Heaven is described in detail in the Bible. Heaven is a place where all things are spiritual, immortal, powerful, and glorious (1 Cor. 15:42-44). In heaven, we will eat from the tree of life, which bears twelve different kinds of fruit and whose leaves are for the "healing of the nations" (Rev. 22:1-4). There will be no more night, and God will "wipe away all tears from their eyes; and there shall be no more death, neither sorrow, nor crying" (Rev. 21:4). God will dwell right there with us, and we will see His face (Rev. 22:4).

Above all, the Bible says, heaven will be a place where God and Jesus are worshiped and where His believers will reign with Him forever and ever.

Will we remember our old life on earth? In Isaiah 65:17, the prophet says that God will create a new heaven and a new earth and "the former shall not be remembered, nor come into mind." Does he mean that we won't remember our lives on earth, our relatives, our friends, our deeds? Perhaps. However, it could also mean we won't remember the bad things that crippled or pained us in our earthly life.

WHO GOES TO HEAVEN?

According to Old Testament scripture, all those who believe in God and His name will go to heaven. "The just shall live by His faith" (Hab. 2:4). It's through faith that the good will find everlasting life.

This New Testament verse is a famous one: "For God so loved the world, that He gave His only begotten Son, that whoever believeth in Him should not perish, but have everlasting life" (John 3:16). The Bible says that belief in Jesus—with your heart, soul, mind, and might—is enough to gain eternal life.

WHAT DOES THE BIBLE SAY ABOUT ANGELS?

The word "angel" means "messenger." Before God made the rest of the universe, He created angels. They are highly intelligent spirit beings originally created to share heaven's glories and to worship and to know God. When Satan rebelled, two-thirds of the angels stood with God and remain with Him to this day (Rev. 12:4). To us they are invisible, but they are able to take human form (Gen. 18:1-3), and they are also able to appear in a visible angelic form that seems but is not human (John 20:12). They accompanied Jesus' birth, temptation in the wilderness, and ascension (Luke 2:8-14; Matt. 4:1-11; Acts 1:10-11). They can appear in dreams (Matt. 1:20). They help, protect, guide, and rescue God's people (Gen. 19:11; Acts 5:19). They perform God's will against nations and peoples—one angel slew 185,000 Assyrians on one occasion (2 Kings 19:35). They do not marry and never die (Luke 20:34-36). They are God's servants and His special ministers to His people (Heb. 1:14).

Probably the most remarkable thing about angels is that the Bible says they can walk among us in human guise, observe us, and even aid people in the midst of distress, and we see them simply as other people. Hebrews 13:2 tells us, "Be not forgetful to entertain strangers: for thereby some have entertained angels unawares." Abraham never knew that he had conversed with an angel (Gen. 18) and Jacob was visited by an angel and only later learned that he had been talking with a messenger from God (Gen 32). But many of us may have spoken, eaten with, or entertained an angel without knowing it. How could we discern whether that person was an angel? Perhaps by the help they rendered, the questions they asked, or the goodness they displayed—but the book of Hebrews says we probably will never know.

WHAT DOES THE BIBLE SAY ABOUT DEMONS AND DEVILS?

"Devil" means "slanderer" in Greek, and "Demon" means "evil spirit." Taken as generic terms, they are used interchangeably, though one connotes activity—slandering God, Jesus, and God's people—and the other connotes a state of existence or spirit.

Demons and devils are evil spirits. They were once angels in heaven but rebelled under the leadership of Satan against God (Rev. 12:9). They are invisible, but they can possess a human who is open to a demon's power (Matt. 8:28-34). In some cases, the Bible says they took human form and mated with women. The result was a progeny of giants who ruled the earth and became a scourge to God. These demons were banished to the Pit of Darkness because of their disobedience, but God sent the Great Flood to rid the world of those giants.

Demons have wrought in the world a multitude of evil deeds. Each wanders throughout the earth looking for those "whom he may devour" (1 Pet. 5:8). They tempt people through planting ideas and thoughts in their minds (Matt. 4:1-11). However, they do not have the power to know our thoughts unless we communicate them; demons are not omniscient. They are powerful, highly intellectual, and intelligent but are not singly or corporately greater than God. They tempt, deceive, slander, accuse, hate, and revile anyone aligned with God and Jesus.

The Bible teaches us about demons so we will be aware of the power of the spirit world. Paul said that "we wrestle not against flesh and blood, but against the principalities, against powers, against the rulers of the darkness of this world, against spiritual wickedness in high places" (Eph. 6:12). Thus, we can be sure that the real battle is not so much against other humans as against the spiritual forces which control and guide evil people.

WHO IS SATAN?

"Satan" means "adversary" or "one who opposes." In that respect, Satan won his name by opposing God, the creator of the heavens and the earth. Some people interpret Isaiah 14:12-14, and Ezekiel 28:11-19, in conjunction with Matthew 4:1-11 and much of Revelation, to mean that Satan was originally Lucifer ("shining one"), the highest archangel God ever created. He was once the covering cherub, an angel with four wings and four faces who protected the holiness of God. Out of pride and jealousy, Lucifer rebelled against God's rule and sought to set up his own kingdom, populated with a third of the angels of heaven who rebelled with him (Rev. 12:4).

God cast him out of heaven and onto the earth. There, the Bible says, he and his cohorts tempt, accuse, deceive, fight, and devour men, women, and children. The Apostle John said that the "whole world lieth in wickedness" (I John 5:19), but Jesus assured us that we should not fear, for

46

"greater is He that is in you, than he that is in the world" (1 John 4:4).

The Bible says that God allows Satan and his rebels to have limited but broad power in the world to tempt and test people. In some cases, God allows Satan to use great power over people (Job 1 and 2). But Satan is always entirely under the rule of God and can do nothing unless God in His sovereignty permits it. Ultimately, Satan will be chained in hell forever (Rev. 20). He will never again tempt or mislead peoples or nations, and the new universe will be marked by equity, justice, goodness, and righteousness.

WHAT WILL HELL BE LIKE?

Scripture speaks of hell frequently. Jesus said that it's a place of "weeping and gnashing of teeth" and "where the fire is not quenched" (Matt. 8:12; Mark 9). Revelation 20:14 tells us that hell is a "lake of fire" that never burns out. It's called "the second death."

Hell will be a place where evildoers are kept alone so that they cannot harm anyone—even their fellow prisoners in hell—again. They will have bodies that can feel thirst, hunger, sexual desire, and pain, but they will not have anything with which to satisfy their desires. It will be a place of utter darkness (Jude 13) that will be impenetrable and constant. The Bible uses many similar terms to mark hell's eternal nature: "everlasting punishment" (Matt. 25:46), "everlasting destruction" (2 Thess. 1:9), the "bottomless pit" (Rev. 9:2,11), and "outer darkness" (Matt. 8:12).

The purpose of hell is judgment, its duration is eternal, and its condition is a state of complete sin and unrighteousness. Those thrown into the "pit" will be utterly bereft of the presence, kindness, joy, and fellowship of God.

WHAT DOES THE BIBLE SAY ABOUT THE CREATION?

In the Bible, Genesis 1-2 lays out a description of how God created heaven, earth, vegetation, animals, and people. This is a not a scientific rendering of how God actually created these things. Genesis 1:3, 6, 9, 14, 20, and 24 all indicate that God merely "spoke" the word, and the world came to be—the sun, stars, earth, light, darkness, sea, and all that is. Scientists and theologians argue about the meaning of these words and whether they are meant to portray a literal description of historical events.

Perhaps the best summary of how believers view the mysteries of creation is stated in Hebrews 11:3: "through faith we understand that the worlds were framed by the word of God, so that things which are seen were not made of things which do appear."

As for human life, according to Genesis 2:7 God first created Adam out of the Middle East's red "dust of the ground," or "adamah" in Hebrew. God breathed life into his nostrils, and the man called Adam, which means "blood" or "red" in Hebrew, walked and talked in fellowship and harmony with God. All through the different periods of creation, when God was done with His work, He pronounced a benediction over His efforts, saying, "It is good." However, when He finished creating Adam, He said, "It is not good that the man should be alone; I will make him an helpmate for him" (Gen. 2:18).

God put Adam into a deep sleep, took out one of his ribs, and fashioned Eve from it. ("Eve" means "life" in Hebrew.) When Adam awakened, God brought the two together and Adam cried, "This is now bone of my bones, and flesh of my flesh: she shall be called Woman, because she was taken out of Man" (Gen. 2:23). Thus, they were two parts of a whole.

WHAT DOES THE BIBLE SAY ABOUT BAPTISM?

The Greek word for baptism is *bapto,* meaning "to dip" as into water. Many scholars believe that the baptisms done by John the Baptist, Jesus' disciples, and the early church were immersions into bodies of water. According to Matthew 3:6, all the people in the district around the Jordan River were "baptized of him in Jordan, confessing their sins." It would seem that if they were being baptized—i.e., "dipped"—in the Jordan River that they must have been immersed—plunged into and entirely covered by the water.

Later in Matthew, when Jesus was baptized, these words were written: "And Jesus, when He was baptized, went up straightway out of the water. . ." (Matt. 3:16). Again, it appears straightforward. How could Jesus go "straightway out" of the water if he wasn't "in" it?

Other scholars argue that the same word that means "dipped" in certain places also means "washed" or "cleansed," especially in the Old Testament usage. These scholars, therefore, prefer sprinkling as the mode of baptism, and this is the most prevalent mode in the Christian church today. Roman Catholics, Presbyterians, Episcopalians, Congregationalists, and many others practice sprinkling instead of immersion.

Regardless of the kind of baptism one undergoes, the primary point is what it signifies. John the Baptist preached a "baptism of repentance." It represented cleansing, internally, spiritually, and emotionally.

Jesus went further, identifying baptism as a picture of being "born again" (John 3). Baptism outwardly demonstrated the internal transformation. But Paul the Apostle took the idea a step further. In Romans 6:3-5, Paul wrote that baptism—being dipped into the water and coming up again—represented our identification with Christ in His death and resurrection. Thus, when we are baptized, we are buried with Christ in His death, and raised again to new life through His resurrection.

All the forms of baptism used in the church today—immersion, sprinkling, and effusion (pouring water out of a cup onto your head)—represent elements of this single act. Immersion shows our death with Christ and our rising again with Him to new life. Sprinkling shows the cleansing and the act of being "dyed" or "changed" so that we are new people in Christ. Effusion pictures the "pouring out" of the Holy Spirit upon the new believer so that he or she is animated and filled with divine power. These ordinances are all based on strong and long-held traditions in the various churches that employ them. The specific mode of baptism does not seem to be the Bible's or God's concern; rather, it's the act of repentance and faith. Baptism represents the individual's new stance and commitment to Christ, to the church, and to God's people.

The only remaining question is: who should be baptized? Some traditions believe that only those who have reached an age where they can understand what they're doing should be baptized. This means children under the age of four or five probably should not be baptized. The predominant tradition practiced in the church today is "infant baptism." Usually the infant is sprinkled with water, representing his or her inclusion in the covenant as the son or daughter of believers. This tradition is based on the early teaching of the church under St. Augustine and others who held that baptism in the New Testament was similar to circumcision in the Old Testament. Circumcision was performed on Jewish boys at the age of eight days, and it signified inclusion, protection, and all the rights and privileges of being under God's rule and love. Infant baptism reflected the same idea. A newborn required the protection and power of God's care.

WHAT DOES THE BIBLE SAY ABOUT THE MESSIAH?

Messiah is the Greek form of the Hebrew word that means "the anointed one." "Christ" is the English transcription of the Greek translation of "messiah." Anointing signified the special gift of the Spirit and of the grace to accomplish an important mission, ministry or deed. Lucifer was called the "anointed cherub" in Ezekiel 28. David was "anointed" with oil as king of Israel by Samuel when he was still a teenager.

However, the "anointed one" occupied a special place in Jewish history. A special "anointed one" was to bring peace to Israel and to rule all the nations with a rod of iron. He would be king over this future kingdom and rule forever and ever. He would be the first "righteous" king to rule and His kingdom would have no end.

In the Old Testament, a "messiah" is also pictured as the suffering servant of the Lord who will reconcile God's people to God the Father. Isaiah 53 is the best picture of this, offering us a scene in which this messiah will suffer and die, be afflicted and "smitten" in our place. Thus, this messiah could be seen both as a king and as a suffering servant who died for the sins of the world.

However, many Jews rejected this image, not equating the kingly elements of the special messiah with the suffering elements of the messiah. Certain New Testament passages imply that the Jews rejected Jesus because He not only did not bring in the kingdom, but because He appeared rough, unlearned, and a nonconformist.

Ultimately, both the Old and New Testaments view the Messiah as a formidable person who will herald and assure the kingdom of God in the new heavens and earth. He is our Master, our King, our friend, our brother, and our savior all in one. The children of Israel await his coming, and Christians expect His second coming.

CHAPTER FOUR

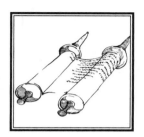

WHAT ARE SOME INTERESTING FACTS IN THE BIBLE?

WHO WERE THE TWELVE TRIBES OF ISRAEL?

Jacob, the son of Isaac and Rebekah, was the father of twelve sons and one daughter, Dinah. The sons became the heads of the twelve tribes of Israel. Jacob's two wives, the sisters Leah and Rachel, were very jealous of one another.

Jacob truly loved Rachel, but the girls' father, Laban, had tricked him into marrying Leah first because she was the older. Leah produced the first sons, and they were, in order of birth, Reuben, Simeon, Levi, and Judah. Rachel was barren. But Rachel gave Jacob her handmaiden Bilhah, so that through her Rachel might have children. Bilhah promptly produced Dan and Naphtali.

At that point, Leah gave Jacob her handmaiden, Zilpah, and this woman gave him two more sons, Gad and Asher. Leah then negotiated with Rachel so that she could lie with Jacob again, and Rachel agreed. Leah conceived and gave birth to two more sons, Issachar and Zebulun.

Finally, after all this time, God had mercy upon Rachel and she gave birth to two sons, Joseph and Benjamin.

Then, Leah conceived once more and this time gave Jacob a daughter, Dinah.

Thus, you can see the lineage looks like this:

Leah	(1) Reuben
	(2) Simeon
	(3) Levi
	(4) Judah—line of Jesus
	(9) Issachar
	(10) Zebulun
Bilhah—handmaid of Rachel	(5) Dan
	(6) Naphtali
Zilpah—handmaid of Leah	(7) Gad
	(8) Asher
Rachel	(11) Joseph
	(12) Benjamin

In ancient times, all Jews were able to trace their lineage to one of these twelve tribes. In the days of Jesus, a person's lineage was traced all the way back to these tribes (as with Joseph's in Matthew 1 and Mary's in Luke 3). Some books of the Bible, such as Numbers, and 1 and 2 Chronicles, contain long lists of lineage from these twelve tribes.

WHAT HAPPENED TO THE LOST TRIBES OF ISRAEL?

After the reign of King Solomon, in 930 B.C., the nation of Israel split into two factions: the Northern Kingdom, which is also called Israel, consisted of ten tribes, and the Southern Kingdom, which is also called Judah, consisted of two tribes. These two kingdoms continued independently of one another until each was conquered and carried into exile.

The Bible says that God warned the Northern Kingdom to stop their sins of idolatry, extortion, murder, and adultery. God's punishment came in the form of total defeat when the Jews were conquered by the Assyrians in 722 B.C. Sargon II, king of Assyria, deported tens of thousands of the northern Jews and replaced them with foreign colonists, destroying the existing Jewish culture and community. When Sargon II removed most of the people of these tribes from their homelands, he made many slaves and subjected all to Assyrian rule. The ultimate fate of most of these people is unknown, hence they came to be known as the lost tribes of the nation of Israel.

WHAT WAS THE ARK
OF THE COVENANT?

The ark was the central object in Israelite worship. It represented the presence of God, and in the early days of Israel the "cloud" of the presence and the "Shekinah glory" of God rested on it in the portable shrine called the "tent of meeting." The Bible relates that the ark was made of acacia wood and was covered with pure gold. On the top, cherubim at each end were configured with wings that spread and arched over the mercy seat. On the side of each end, two golden rings adorned the ark, through which two staves covered in gold were placed for carrying. The ark was always to be carried by priests holding these staves or poles. It was never to be transported by cart or other means (Ex. 25-28).

God ordered that three things be placed inside the ark: the stone tablets on which the Ten Commandments were written; a golden jar holding manna or bread; and Aaron's rod, which had budded almond blossoms during an early episode when Israel challenged Aaron's authority and position (Num. 17).

The ark stood in the Holy of Holies, the deepest sanctum of the tabernacle for worship. No one saw this ark except for the high priest, and he saw it only on the most sacred of the ceremonial occasions. An elaborate veil stood between the Holy of Holies and the Holy Place, the outer room where sacrifices took place. This represented God's separation from the people because of sin.

In Scripture, all the elements of temple worship were representative of heavenly realities. Thus, the ark spoke of God's abiding presence with His people and of His mercy and forgiving love toward sinners.

When the temple was destroyed in 586 B.C. by the Babylonians, the ark disappeared and was never seen again.

WHAT IS A SAINT IN SCRIPTURE?

Contrary to popular belief, saints in Scripture are not the same ones designated by the church. To be heralded as a saint in church lore, one must perform substantiated miracles and meet a number of other qualifications. In Scripture, this was not so.

"Saint," derived from a Greek word meaning "sanctified" or "holy one," primarily signifies one who is set apart for God's purposes.

The result is that in the New Testament every person who puts his or her faith in Christ is considered a saint. All Christians are separated for God's service and worship. Thus, 1 Corinthians 1:1-2 states: "Paul. . . Unto the church of God which is at Corinth, to them that are sanctified in Christ Jesus, called to be saints. . . ."

WHAT IS GOD CALLED
IN THE BIBLE?

In the Bible, God reveals Himself through His names and attributes. Each name or attribute represents some truth or principle about Him. Some believers count sixteen names that God reveals for Himself in the Old Testament. They are:

Adonai—means "Lord," representing God's Lordly relationship with us (Mal. 1:6).

Jehovah—a word used for Yahweh, which shows God's salvation (Gen. 2:4).

Elohim—God's power and might and thus His ability to protect us (Gen. 1:1).

Jehovah-Shammah—"The Lord is there," showing that God is there for us when we need Him (Ezek. 48:35).

Jehovah-Rohi—"The Lord is my shepherd," demonstrating God's leadership and guidance (Ps. 23:1).

Jehovah-Maccaddeshem—"The Lord that doth sanctify you," speaking of the fact that He transforms and consecrates us (Exod. 31:13).

Jehovah-Rapha—"The Lord thy healer," signifying His power to heal and help (Exod. 15:26).

Jehovah-Sabbaoth—"The Lord of hosts" or armies, picturing His power to rescue and fight on our behalf (Isa. 6:1-3).

Jehovah-jireh—"The Lord who provides," explicating His ability to provide (Gen. 22:13-14).

Jehovah-Tsidkenu—"The Lord our righteousness,"

showing that He Himself is righteous and good on our behalf (Jer. 23:6).

Jehovah-nissi—"The Lord our banner,"showing that God leads us into battle and goes ahead of us (Exod. 17:15).

Jehovah-shalom—"The Lord is peace," signifying that God gives us peace (Judg. 6:24).

El-Elyon—"The most high God," demonstrating that He is utterly holy and high over us in power and esteem (Gen. 14:17-20).

El-Shaddai—"Almighty God," showing that He is the almighty God (Gen. 17:1).

El-Roi—"God sees," proving that He knows our plight and is strong to save (Gen. 16:13).

El-Olam—"The everlasting God," pointing out that He will never die (Isa. 40:28).

As you can see, each of these names represents something significant and important about God's relationship with the people in the Bible. In modern times, they can be considered a measure of our relationship with Him. When we are in trouble, we might call on El-Roi, God who sees all, in prayer and ask for help. When we are sick, we cry out to Jehovah-Rapha, God our healer. The names in this respect become an aid to worship. But their substance is the same.

WHAT DID "JEHOVAH" MEAN TO THE HEBREWS?

Jews practiced the law and felt strongly about the third commandment: "thou shalt not take the name of the Lord thy God in vain." Thus, they were careful not to pronounce God's primary name, "Yahweh," with disdain or mockery or perhaps at all. When rabbis read from the texts of the Bible or other documents, they did not pronounce Yahweh when they came to that name. Instead, they substituted the Hebrew word, "Adonai," which means "Lord." Eventually Jews came to understand that the name Yahweh was sacred and it became forbidden for a Jew to pronounce the name "Yahweh," or they would suffer stoning.

Later, when the Masoretes, the scribes who copied the scriptures after A.D. 400, came upon the letters YHWH (called the "tetragrammaton" or "four letters" of the Name), they inserted the vowels of Adonai, which in Hebrew are the equivalent of E-O-A, under the consonants YHWH. Thus, through the blending of the two words the word became YeHoWaH—"Jehovah" in Hebrew pronunciation.

"Yahweh," the name of names, the primary name of God as revealed to Moses by the burning bush (Exod. 3:14) means, "I am that I am." Thus, it represents God's self-existence: "I am the one who exists above and beyond all others." "I am the one who exists on His own; I am not dependent on any other." While people are born into this world, God said that He was never born, He has always been. People need food, water, and sustenance to exist. But God requires nothing. God is self-existing.

WERE THE GREAT FLOOD
AND NOAH'S ARK REAL?

As with many biblical teachings, the flood generates infinite speculation, argument, and interest. Some claim the flood was universal—covering the whole earth. Others believe it was confined to the Middle East.

Scripture relates that mankind degenerated from the creation into a state of such sin that God decided to destroy all life on earth. He gave mankind 120 years to repent and to turn back to Him in faith. He saw only one family on the face of the earth worth preserving: Noah, his wife, his three sons, and their wives. God commissioned Noah to build an ark in which Noah and his family and pairs of animals would be protected during the flood.

Noah built the ark over the next 120 years. Presumably, it was a project that attracted much attention. Noah preached to the onlookers and offered them hope through repentance. His words were not heard, though, and only Noah's family survived.

One piece of information found in Genesis 6:15 is the dimensions of the ark: length, 300 cubits (a cubit is about eighteen inches); breadth, fifty cubits; height, thirty cubits—the approximate size of a modern cargo ship.

While many argue about the extent of the flood, one fact remains: more than 270 stories in different cultures around the world repeat tales like that of the Great Flood.

CHAPTER FIVE

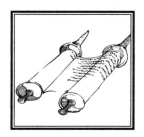

WHAT MIRACLES OCCUR IN THE BIBLE?

WHAT IS A MIRACLE?

A miracle is any event or experience that defies natural order and is clearly the result of supernatural intervention. The basic elements are the words "supernatural," meaning beyond the natural, and "intervention," which relates action on a divine scale. If grape juice which is put into a wineskin ferments naturally into wine, no one is amazed. But when a jug filled with water from the well has turned at Jesus' command to wine—in taste, texture, quantity, and power to intoxicate—that is a miracle. If a blind person submits to a cornea transplant operation so that he or she can see again, that is modern medicine. But if a man who was born blind cries out to Jesus to make him see, and Jesus says, "Be it done to you as you have believed," and the man regains his sight, that is a miracle. Miracles are sudden, complete, unequivocal, and simple. Natural events follow natural processes. A miracle happens when an outside force or person invades the natural and does something supernatural.

The Bible gives countless examples of how God has responded to the prayers of His people with miracles. Hezekiah, the king, prayed that God would stop Sennacherib's 185,000 soldiers from taking Jerusalem. God sent an angel who slew His enemies.

The Book of Jonah contains a number of individual miracles: the supernatural storm thrown on the sea by God to stop Jonah; Jonah's rescue from drowning by being swallowed by a great fish; the supernatural conversion of the Ninevites when Jonah preached to them; and the supernatural growth of the shading gourd as well as its withering. These were separate and unique miracles that God performed for a singular purpose.

WERE MIRACLES EVER COMMON?

There are many miracles related in the Old Testament. One of the most dramatic sequences of miracles occurred in the time of Moses. As Moses struggled with Pharaoh to release his people, God showed his awful power to Pharaoh and the people of Egypt. God afflicted Egypt with ten plagues, each more horrible than the next, that forced the Israelites' release. As Moses and his people fled into the wilderness, God parted the Red Sea to allow His chosen people to escape, and He caused the sea to crash in over the Egyptian troops as they followed. This journey in the wilderness saw many of God's miracles. God took form so that His people could understand, appearing in a cloud by day and a pillar of fire by night. God provided for His people in the desert by giving them manna or bread each morning, and He punished them by supernatural events when they tried His patience.

The prophetic times of Elijah and Elisha were also rich with miracles. Elijah prayed, and God withheld rain for three years in Israel. To test God's strength, Elijah asked God to send a lightning bolt to consume a sacrifice. God's bolt consumed not only the sacrifice, but its altar and the water in the moat around it, which convinced many pagan people of God's supreme power. Elisha's miracles were more personal: he raised a boy from the dead, made a metal axe head float, and saved people from poisoned food.

The last record of miracles came during Jesus' ministry and in the works of the early Christian church.

DID JESUS PERFORM MIRACLES?

The New Testament gospels are a narrative recounting of the miracles of Jesus and His disciples. The first four books of the New Testament delineate thirty-five separate miracles that Jesus performed. One kind of miracle was the healing of illness. Jesus healed blind, deaf, mute, and crippled people of every imaginable kind. The miracles were instantaneous and unchangeable. The lame walked. The blind saw. The deaf heard. The leper was made healthy.

A second kind of miracle was the casting out of demons. On a number of occasions, Jesus cast out one or many demons from individuals who were immediately changed for the better.

A third kind of miracle was the performance of a miraculous act to help others, such as changing water into wine at Cana, feeding the multitudes with loaves and fish, and finding the tax money in the fish's mouth.

A fourth kind of miracle was raising the dead. Jesus raised three dead people—the widow of Nain's son (Luke 7:11-15); the daughter of Jairus (Luke 8:40-56); and Lazarus (John 11:17-44).

The last kind was the stupendous, awe-inspiring miracle, of which Jesus performed only a few: stilling the storm, giving Peter a miraculous catch of fish, and walking on water.

The Scriptures state clearly that these were not the limits of Jesus' miracles. Rather, these thirty-five are the ones written about in detail. Jesus performed multitudes of other miracles that are just mentioned in passing. In Matthew 4:23 it says: "And Jesus went about all Galilee, teaching in their synagogues, and preaching the gospel of the kingdom, and healing all manner of sickness and all manner of disease among the people." That verse might account for hundreds of specific deeds that are lost to history.

WHAT ARE HIS
BEST KNOWN MIRACLES?

Changing water into wine at Cana (John 2:1-11).

The healing of a lame man who did not ask for healing, by the pool of Bethesda (John 5:1-9).

Cleansing a leper who asked for healing (Matt. 8:2-4).

Healing a paralytic (Matt. 9:2-4).

Raising the son of the widow of Nain in the middle of his funeral procession (Luke 7:11-15).

Stilling a storm on the Sea of Galilee (Mark 4:35-41).

Casting demons out of the Gadarene demoniacs (Mark 5:1-20).

Feeding the 5,000 (John 6:5-13).

Walking on water during a storm (Matt. 14:24-33).

Delivering a demon-possessed boy who had stymied His disciples (Mark 9:14-29).

Peter finding the tax money in the mouth of the fish (Matt. 17:24-27).

Raising Lazarus from the dead (John 11:17-44).

Healing ten lepers, only one of whom thanked Jesus (Luke 17:11-19).

Restoring the ear of the priest's servant that Peter had cut off (John 18:10).

WHO DECIDES THAT
A MIRACLE HAS OCCURRED?

The church has always had certain tests by which it determines whether an act is a miracle. These tests, admittedly, are fairly subjective but only those who question the basic veracity of the Bible dispute that it contains records of miracles. The tests by which miracles are determined are:

1) Was it seen by witnesses? Will those who saw it happen give testimony to the fact that a miracle has occurred?

2) Was the situation prior to the miracle natural and longstanding? Was the blind man known to be blind for many months or years? Was the sea in a state of storm? Was the person proven dead and ready for the grave?

3) Did the miracle change the person or thing permanently? The blind man sees for the rest of his life; the leper is healed thereafter.

4) Did the person who performed the miracle (or prayed for it) claim it was God's power or his own? Only those who recognize God's power as the essential ingredient can claim to have participated in a miracle.

If all four of these tests are answered in the positive, the church can assert that what took place was a true miracle.

CHAPTER SIX

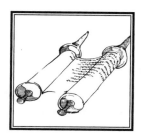

WHAT ARE THE PROPHECIES OF THE BIBLE?

WHO WERE THE PROPHETS?

A prophet was God's spokesman. The Greek word for prophet meant "forthteller," one who spoke for God and revealed His will. A prophet received a specific "call" from God. That is, God revealed Himself to the prophet in a vision or dream or by other means and called him to specific work. Moses was the first prophet, though the Bible mentions that before him others such as Lamech, Enoch, Abraham, Isaac, and Jacob spoke prophetic words. However, they are not considered prophets in the classic sense.

As the first major prophet, Moses both "forthtold" and "foretold." He explained the word of God to God's people, and he predicted certain events that would come to pass. Moses was called by God at the burning bush (Exod. 3:2), and God commissioned him to lead the people of Israel out of slavery.

The test of a true prophet was truth. If events unfolded as they predicted, then the people recognized a true prophet called by God. But all the words had to come true—at least those that predicted the immediate future. If a biblical prophet gave an inaccurate prediction, the prophet was considered false, and his life would end by stoning or another means of execution.

WHAT WAS A FALSE PROPHET?

A false prophet was anyone who claimed to have God's anointing and the power to predict the future, but who was not truly selected by God. How would you know a false prophet? Deuteronomy 18:22 puts it this way: "When a prophet speaketh in the name of the Lord, if the thing follow not, nor come to pass, that is the thing which the Lord hath not spoken, but the prophet hath spoken it presumptuously: thou shalt not be afraid of him."

WHO WERE THE MAJOR
AND MINOR PROPHETS?

Jewish tradition divided all other Old Testament prophets into two categories: the major and the minor prophets. The major prophets were called "major" because of the length of the books associated with their names, not because they were better or more important. The major prophets are Isaiah, Jeremiah, and Ezekiel.

Sometimes called "the twelve," the minor prophets were described in short books of the Bible. The minor prophets are Hosea, Joel, Amos, Obadiah, Jonah, Micah, Nahum, Habakkuk, Zephaniah, Haggai, Zechariah, and Malachi.

Daniel is not considered one of the prophets, but a historian. He is included in the "writings."

WHICH PROPHECIES FORESAW THE
COMING OF A MESSIAH?

There are many Messianic prophecies in Scripture, largely of two types. One line of prophecy predicts a kingly, conquering Messiah who would bring eternal righteousness, peace, and love. The book of Isaiah especially speaks of this Messiah. In the King James translation, Isaiah 9:6-7 says:

For unto us a child is born, unto us a son is given;
and the government shall be upon His shoulder:

71

and His name shall be called Wonderful, Counsellor,
  The mighty God,
The Everlasting Father, The Prince of Peace.
Of the increase of His government and peace there
  shall be no end,
upon the throne of David, and upon his kingdom,
to order it, and to establish it with judgment and
  with justice
from henceforth even for ever.
The zeal of the Lord of Hosts will perform this.

Words like government, throne, and kingdom indicate the power and courtliness of the coming Messiah. Another wonderful description of this element of the Messiah's purpose and deportment comes from Isaiah 42:1-3:

Behold, My servant, whom I uphold;
Mine elect, in whom My soul delighteth;
I have put My spirit upon Him:
He shall bring forth judgment to the Gentiles.
He shall not cry, nor lift up,
nor cause His voice to be heard in the street.
A bruised reed shall He not break,
and the smoking flax shall He not quench:
He shall bring forth judgment unto truth.
He shall not fail nor be discouraged,
till He have set judgment in the earth:
and the isles shall wait for His law.

On the other hand, prophecies about a suffering Messiah seem to pose a contradiction. How could a king, a Lord, a Master, suffer? The words of Isaiah 53:2-3 state:

For He shall grow up before Him as a tender plant,
and as a root out of a dry ground:
He hath no form nor comeliness; and
when we shall see Him,
there is no beauty that we should desire Him.
He is despised and rejected of men;
a man of sorrows, and acquainted with grief:
and we hid as it were our faces from Him;
He was despised, and we esteemed Him not. "

The passage goes on to speak of a grieving Messiah, whom God "wounded for our transgressions," and who is "bruised for our iniquities." He was "brought as a lamb to the slaughter" and "He made His grave with the wicked." Many think this passage pictures Jesus' first coming.

WERE THERE OTHER PROPHECIES ABOUT JESUS?

By some Christian scholars' accounting, there are more than 300 prophecies in the Old Testament that were fulfilled by Jesus in His first coming. Some of these are precise predictions that specify exactly what would happen and make it clear that they are about Jesus the Messiah. For instance, throughout history God spoke of the specific people through whose lineage the Messiah would come. He says this of Eve, Shem, the son of Noah, Abraham, Isaac and Jacob, and Judah, the fourth son of Jacob. Throughout history God narrows it and narrows it until we get a very precise picture of the Messiah. Few people in history could fit this family line.

Other prophecies are "types." That is, they are events or situations that happened to Israel or others, but that find fulfillment in Jesus. For instance, when God told Abraham to sacrifice Isaac, it appeared a simple enough act. But, in fact, it was a prototype of something to come: God sacrificing His own son in the place of others. Types of prophecy are found all through Scripture and range from the simple—Israel coming out of Egypt as Jesus came out of Egypt after fleeing from Herod as a boy—to the sublime: Jonah in the belly of the fish for three days and three nights, as Jesus would be in the belly of the earth for the same period of time.

Several prophecies that Jesus fulfilled are:

1. He would in some special way be born of a woman—Gen. 3:15.
2. He would be from the line of Abraham—Gen 12:3
3. He would be from the line of Judah—Gen. 49:10.
4. He would be born of a virgin—Isa. 7:14.
5. He would reign on the throne of David—2 Sam 7:11-12.
6. He would be called "Immanuel," "God with us"—Isa. 7:14.
7. He would be born in Bethlehem—Mic. 5:2.
8. He would be worshiped by wise men and they would give Him gifts—Ps. 72:10-11.
9. He would spend time in Egypt in His early days—Num. 24:8.
10. Someone would massacre babies from His birth place—Jer. 31:15.

11. He would be called "despised"—Isa. 53:3;
    Psalms 22:6.
12. He would heal many—Isa. 53:5.
13. He would speak in parables—Isa. 6:9-10.
14. He would be rejected—Isa. 53:3.
15. He would enter Jerusalem in triumph—Zech. 9:9.
16. His miracles wouldn't be believed—Isa. 53:1.
17. A friend would betray Him for 30 pieces of silver—
    Zech. 11:12-13.
18. He would be crucified between two thieves—
    Isa. 53:12.
19. His hands and feet would be pierced—Ps. 22:16.
20. Soldiers would gamble for His garments—
    Ps. 22:18.
21. None of His bones would be broken—Exod. 12:46;
    Ps. 34:20.
22. His burial place would be a rich man's tomb—
    Isa. 53:9.
23. He would rise from the dead—Ps. 16:10.
24. He would ascend into heaven visibly—
    Ps. 24:7-10.

CHAPTER SEVEN

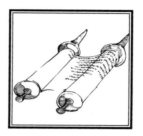

WHO WAS JESUS?

WHAT IS JESUS' ROLE IN THE BIBLE?

"Jesus" is the Greek form of the Hebrew name Joshua. It means "Jehovah is salvation." "Christ" is the Greek word for Messiah, which means "the anointed one."

The Bible relates that Jesus Christ was an itinerant preacher, healer, and miracle worker during the first half of the first century A.D. His ministry began when He was about thirty years old and spanned three and a half years. One way of understanding the Gospels is that, though He was very popular with the common people, the reigning religious leaders perceived Jesus as a great threat to their religion and the business that accrued from their religious beliefs. They eventually snared Him, and tried to discredit Him. The Romans crucified Him (which was the standard form of Roman execution in those days). However, on the third day after His execution, Jesus rose from the dead and appeared to His disciples for 40 days at various times and places. At the end of 40 days, He bodily and visibly ascended into heaven. Ten days later, as He had predicted, His spirit was poured out on His disciples and followers; and, beginning from Jerusalem, they spread the news about His life, death, and resurrection to the rest of the world.

WHERE AND WHEN WAS JESUS BORN?

Although the calendar naturally puts the birth of Christ in A.D. 0, archaeology and other resources have found that Jesus must have been born somewhere between 6 and 4 B.C. This coincides with the last days of the murderous Herod the Great, who was threatened by the knowledge of the coming of the Messiah as revealed to him by the Magi, the wise men who studied the stars and concluded that a special star represented the coming of the Hebrew Messiah.

Jesus was born in Bethlehem of Judea by a series of providential miracles. First, the New Testament relates that His mother Mary had conceived Him through the intervention of the Holy Spirit without sexual relations with a man; she was a virgin. Thus, Jesus was born "without sin" and would live His life perfectly under the hand and direction of God the Father.

Mary and her betrothed husband, Joseph, lived in a northern city, possibly Nazareth in Galilee. They would not normally have traveled to Judea, especially with Mary pregnant and about to give birth, but a decree from Caesar Augustus required that every man return to his ancestral city to register for tax purposes. Mary and Joseph traveled to Bethlehem, and Jesus was born there. It had long been predicted by the prophet Micah that the Messiah would be born in Bethlehem (see Mic. 5:2). Jesus' birth was accompanied by signs in heaven—a special star or perhaps the Shekinah glory of God descending onto the little stable where He dwelled—and by appearances of angels, shepherds, and wise men. Though His beginning was humble— He was born in a stable, wrapped in rags, and laid in a feed trough—it was the perfect means for the Messiah to come into the world. In effect, God was saying that His Son would get no special treatment and He would live as an ordinary man come to save ordinary men and women.

WHO WERE THE MAGI?

The word *magi* refers to a religious caste of astrologers and diviners who originated in Persia, then spread to many other cultures in Arabia. By the time of Christ, magi came to refer to any magician or sorcerer, though the Magi of the Christ birth narratives were clearly not simple magicians.

Some people think the caste of the Magi originated in Babylon. They may have been there when Daniel and the exiled Jews came to Babylon. Daniel might have influenced the group through his ability to interpret dreams and his interest in biblical prophecy. A cult might have begun that looked for the signs that Daniel had said would accompany the arrival of the Jewish Messiah. The beliefs and practices of this cult were passed from one generation to the next, and by Christ's time these magicians and astrologers were eagerly looking for a king Whom they would anoint as the Lord of creation. How much of this they understood is debatable, but it's possible the Magi were "king makers" from the east who desired to give their approval and crest to the Son of God whenever He should come into the world.

Studying the heavens, the Magi saw a special star in the sky and interpreted it as the sign they sought from the prophecies of Balaam (Num. 24:17). They traveled west and visited King Herod's court, where they were informed that the Messiah was to be born in Bethlehem. Herod sent them along, asking them to inform him when they found the Messiah. At Bethlehem they found the baby, worshiped Him, and presented to Him three gifts—gold, frankincense, and myrrh. Frankincense is a gum resin obtained from trees in the balsam family and was used for perfume and medicinal purposes and used by the Jews in religious rites. Myrrh, another gum resin that hardened into red or black globules, was used as a perfume and medicine, and also in burial. After the presentation, the Magi were warned in a dream not to return to Herod, so they left Judea by another route. That there were three Magi, and that they were kings, is a legend that arose in medieval times.

WHERE DID JESUS GROW UP?

Sometime after the death of Herod the Great, an angel appeared to Joseph in a dream. The family was residing in Egypt to escape the persecution that Herod wreaked on Bethlehem after the Magi left without revealing Christ's location. Joseph and his family returned to Judea, but when he learned that Archelaus was reigning in place of his father, Herod, Joseph inquired of God and was sent to Galilee. There he settled in the cosmopolitan city of Nazareth—an important trade center in the north—and set up a carpentry shop. Jesus grew up in Nazareth and one of the spoken prophecies related that He would be called a "Nazarene" (see Matt. 2:23).

The Bible tells us little of Jesus' early years. We only know that when He was twelve, His parents traveled to Jerusalem at Passover. They had done this every year from the time they'd lived in Nazareth to expose Jesus to all the traditions of His people. This time, however, Jesus slipped away and conferred with the great teachers in the temple. After the Passover, His parents discovered He was missing from their little caravan going back to Nazareth. They returned to Jerusalem and found Him in the Temple with the teachers. The teachers found Jesus intelligent, learned in the scriptures, and extremely quick. When His parents confronted Him about not returning with the caravan, Jesus said, "How is it that ye sought Me? Wist ye not that I must be about My Father's business?" (Luke 2:49). He submitted, though, and went home with them.

Obviously, Jesus was an intelligent young man, well-studied in the Scriptures. Presumably He spent much time going over the scrolls in His home town and synagogue. His father also trained Him in carpentry. His later teaching shows that He was familiar with many kinds of occupations in the region, from fishing and boating to local merchant craft and wine-making.

WHEN WAS JESUS FIRST RECOGNIZED AS SPECIAL?

At His baptism. John the Baptist, Jesus' cousin, had called for repentance in light of the coming kingdom of God, and he baptized people as a sign of their belief in his message. Jesus arrived at the Jordan River one day, coming to be baptized like so many others. But John tried to prevent him, saying, "I have need to be baptized of Thee, and comest Thou to me?" But Jesus persuaded him, saying, "For thus it becometh us to fulfill all righteousness" (Matt. 3:14-15).

The Bible relates how John plunged Jesus under the water, and when He burst up, the heavens majestically split open and a voice from heaven said, "This is My beloved Son in Whom I am well pleased" (Matt. 3:17). At that moment, a dove appeared in the air representing the Holy Spirit, and it flew down and rested on Jesus' shoulder, showing that He was now anointed as a prophet to His people. Hundreds, perhaps thousands, of people witnessed this event.

HOW LONG
WAS JESUS' MINISTRY?

Starting with Jesus' baptism and temptation in the wilderness and combining that with the events of John 1 and 2 when Jesus went up to Jerusalem for the Passover, we date the beginning of His ministry about three months before Passover in A.D. 27 or 28. John's Gospel mentions three Passovers—Jesus was crucified at the fourth. This means Jesus' ministry spanned about three and a half years.

WHAT DID JESUS
LOOK LIKE?

All of the many artists' conceptions that portray Jesus have been pure speculation. Nothing in the Gospels describes His appearance outright. Isaiah 53:2 says that He had no "form nor comeliness." It even says He had no "beauty that we should desire Him." Thus, it's possible Jesus was far from the handsome, attractive figure depicted in our world today. It was His divinity, words, and deeds that drew the disciples, not His appearance or personal charm.

WHAT WAS JESUS' CONNECTION TO JOHN THE BAPTIST?

Mary, Jesus' mother, and Elisabeth, John's mother, were cousins, according to Luke 1:36. Thus, John and Jesus were cousins. How much contact they had before Jesus' baptism is unknown. In the Gospels, John does not appear to have known who the Messiah was until Jesus came to be baptized. But since Joseph and Mary traveled to Judea each spring for Passover, and Elisabeth and Zacharias lived in Judea, it's possible they visited. It's possible that John and Jesus played together as boys and even knew one another well before the baptism, but that remains speculation.

HOW DID SATAN TEMPT JESUS IN THE WILDERNESS?

Matthew 4:1 says, "Then was Jesus led up of the Spirit into the wilderness to be tempted of the devil." This temptation was planned and brought about by God the Father and was not happenstance. At least two other instances occur in Scripture of a person fasting for forty days—Moses in Exodus 34:28 and Elijah in 1 Kings 19:8. It was after this period that Jesus became hungry, meaning that He was approaching starvation.

At that point the devil came to Jesus and began a period of temptation. First he challenged Jesus to turn stones into bread, since He had that power. Jesus replied, quoting Deuteronomy 8:3, "Man doth not live by bread only, but by every word that proceedeth out of the mouth of the Lord doth man live."

Satan then proceeded to take Jesus to the top of the temple, and there he quoted Scripture himself. This time he suggested Jesus throw Himself off the tower and then quoted Psalms 91:11–12, leaving out some parts and taking it completely out of context. Again Jesus replied with a counter quote from Deuteronomy 6:16, "Ye shall not tempt the Lord your God."

Undaunted, Satan took Jesus to a high mountain and showed Him all the kingdoms of the world from that height. He said he'd give Jesus all of them if Jesus would just fall down and worship him. Jesus once again paraphrased Old Testament Scripture (Deut. 6:13), saying, "Thou shalt worship the Lord thy God, and Him only shalt thou serve" (Matt. 4:10). At that point, Satan departed, and angels arrived and ministered to Jesus, giving Him food and rest.

This was a formidable temptation. It struck at the very basic elements of Jesus' life and being—flesh, soul, and spirit. Jesus' response shows the power of Scripture in giving response to temptation.

WAS JESUS JEWISH?

Yes. He was born of Jewish parents, both of whom were descended from the lineage of King David, Joseph through Solomon (Matt. 1), and Mary through Nathan (Luke 3).

HOW DID JESUS DIE?

Scripture relates that the Romans crucified Him, naked between two thieves on Golgotha ("Place of the Skull"), a hill outside Jerusalem, before a heckling crowd. All His disciples had run except one, John. Jesus was alone, and it was His crowning and most painful moment.

WHY DID JESUS LET HIMSELF BE KILLED?

The New Testament explains that Jesus came into the world to die for the sins of mankind. Jesus made this clear numerous times. His introduction by John the Baptist was accompanied by John's words, "Behold the Lamb of God which taketh away the sin of the world" (John 1:29). Jesus told His disciples over and over that He came to die so that others might live.

Peter wrote in his Epistle, "Who His own self bare our sins in His own body on the tree, that we, being dead to sins, should live unto righteousness: by whose stripes ye were healed" (1 Peter 2:24).

HOW DO WE KNOW JESUS ROSE FROM THE DEAD?

We have the reports of eyewitnesses. In all four Gospels, Jesus appears numerous times to different people in different places. He eats with them, He talks with them, He lets them touch Him. The disciples were convinced He had risen, and this was the message they took to the people— that Jesus had triumphed over the grave and whoever believed in Him would also rise from the grave.

The power of eyewitness testimony gives powerful insight into historic events. Our courts today depend primarily on eyewitness testimony to convict people of the crimes of which they stand accused. Paul said that after Jesus arose, "He was seen of Cephas [Peter], then of the twelve: After that, He was seen of above 500 brethren at once; of whom the greater part remain unto this present, but some are fallen asleep. After that He was seen of James; then of all the apostles. And last of all He was seen of me also, as of one born out of due time" (1 Cor. 15:5–8).

WHERE WAS JESUS BURIED?

He was buried in Joseph of Arimathea's newly hewn tomb. The Church of the Holy Sepulcher is thought to be built over the site of Jesus' burial, though its authenticity is much disputed. That church was built in A.D. 335 by

Constantine after his mother, Helena, declared the site authentic in A.D. 325. Because of the complete destruction of Jerusalem in A.D. 70, there can be no firm proof that this site is correct.

CHAPTER EIGHT

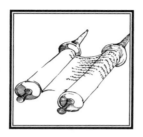

WHAT WERE THE WORDS OF JESUS?

ARE THE WORDS ATTRIBUTED TO JESUS IN THE BIBLE REALLY HIS?

While there is no way to verify if Jesus spoke these words or not, most scholars agree that the Gospels were based on eyewitness accounts. This suggests that these books are, at least in substance, the words of Jesus.

HOW CAN WE INTERPRET JESUS' WORDS?

Scholars have always used specific methods for understanding the intent and meaning of the words of Scripture. One method calls for three areas of consideration: the grammatical meaning, the historical meaning, and the cultural meaning in its context. Considering the meaning from these three perspectives helps us to accurately understand ancient texts.

Jesus spoke to real men and women in a real historical and cultural context. The more we know about history and the culture of the times, the better we can understand His words.

For instance, Jesus quoted the Old Testament in His Sermon on the Mount, citing, "An eye for an eye, and a tooth for a tooth." He then reinterpreted the meaning of that statement, saying, "But I say unto you, That ye resist not evil: but whosoever shall smite thee on thy right cheek, turn to him the other also. And if any man will sue thee at the law, and take away thy coat, let him have thy cloak also. And whosoever shall compel thee to go a mile, go with him twain" (Matt. 5:38–41). In the historical-cultural context, we know that people in early biblical times frequently took the law into their own hands to avenge wrongs. The intent of the biblical law in the original context was that a kinsman or court could not exact more of a punishment than eye for eye and tooth for tooth. Jesus was calling for compassion and mercy. When insulted, don't strike back but turn the other cheek. When you're sued, if you've done wrong, make it right by giving more than required. And if a soldier asked you to carry his equipment for a mile—which was Roman law—then give him more; go two miles. Jesus isn't saying we shouldn't defend ourselves from attack or seek lawful remedies for conflict. He's saying, "Don't take the law into your own hands. Instead, respond graciously."

WHY DID JESUS SAY HE CAME INTO THE WORLD?

The simplest and most definitive statement is found in Luke 19:10: "The Son of Man is come to seek and to save that which was lost."

Jesus often spoke in metaphorical terms. In one place, He said, "I am the way, the truth, and the life: no man cometh unto the Father, but by Me" (John 14:6). In another situation, He said, "I am the light of the world" (John 8:12). And in another, "I am the resurrection, and the life" (John 11:25). Once, Jesus questioned His disciples, asking them who men said He was. They replied that some said He was John the Baptist, others Elijah, and still others said He was one of the prophets. Then Jesus said, "But whom say ye that I am?" Peter replied, "Thou art the Christ, the Son of the living God" (Matt. 16:16). Jesus agreed, saying, "Blessed art thou, Simon Bar-jona: for flesh and blood hath not revealed it unto thee, but My Father which is in heaven."

Elsewhere, the high priest asked Jesus who He was during His trial before the Sanhedrin, the Jews' ruling political and religious body. The high priest said, "I adjure Thee by the living God, that Thou tell us whether Thou be the Christ, the Son of God." Jesus answered, "Thou hast said: nevertheless I say unto you, Hereafter shall ye see the Son of Man sitting on the right hand of power, and coming in the clouds of heaven" (see Matt. 26:63–64). At that point, the high priest accused Him of blasphemy. In the comparison passage in Luke 22:66–71, the priest asked a second question: "Art thou then the Son of God?" And Jesus answered, "Ye say that I am."

From these and many other passages, we see that Jesus claimed to be the Messiah, the Son of God, and therefore God incarnate—God in human flesh.

WHY DID JESUS TELL PARABLES?

Jesus told some thirty different parables, several found in different forms in each of the Gospels. The favorites among them are the "Good Samaritan" (Luke 10:25–37), the "Prodigal Son" (Luke 15:11–32), the "Sower" (Matt. 13:3–8), and "Pearl of Great Price" (Matt. 13:45–46).

Jesus told parables because they were simple ways to explain complex truths. Also, they were interesting, entertaining, and, to some degree, crowd-pleasing. Parables were a traditional method used by rabbis to illustrate truths and abstract concepts.

When Jesus' disciples asked Him why He taught in parables, Jesus answered (Matt. 13:11–13): "Because it is given unto you to know the mysteries of the kingdom of heaven, but to them it is not given. For whosoever hath, to him shall be given, and he shall have more abundance: but whosoever hath not, from him shall be taken away even that he hath. Therefore speak I to them in parables: because they seeing see not; and hearing they hear not, neither do they understand."

What did Jesus mean by this? That those who believed in Him would receive more truth as they grew in faith. Those who rejected Him would think they understood what He was saying, but they wouldn't truly understand.

HOW CAN WE INTERPRET THE PARABLES?

Jesus explained one parable to His disciples, the parable of "The Sower." We can use the same principles to interpret all of the others. All the parables are about Christ's kingdom. The different characters and events represent elements of His kingdom, or elements of the world within the kingdom. They are in this sense mini-allegories, with different people, places, and things representing various real-life people, places, and things. The parable of the lost sheep symbolizes how God feels about one lost person and how He searches throughout the world for that person.

Some parables are more difficult than others, but they're not necessarily meant to be easily understood. People of faith must use their abilities to think, research, ponder, and reason. But most of all, we must use faith to see the spiritual realities in the parables.

WHAT ARE JESUS' SERMONS?

Jesus' sermons in the Gospels are:

The Sermon on the Mount—Matt. 5–7.

The Mission of the Twelve—Matt. 9:35–11:1.

The Parables by the Sea—Matt. 13:1–52.

Message on Humility—Matt. 18.

Denunciations of Hypocrisy—Matt. 23.

The Olivet Discourse (delivered on the Mount of Olives)—Matt. 24–25.

The Upper Room Discourse—John 13–17.

WHAT ARE SOME OF JESUS' FAMOUS SAYINGS?

There are many. Some favorites are:

"Blessed are the poor in spirit: for theirs is the kingdom of heaven" (Matt. 5:3).

"Ye are the salt of the earth" (Matt. 5:13).

"Ye are the light of the world" (Matt. 5:14).

"Pray ye: Our Father which art in heaven, Hallowed be Thy name. Thy kingdom come. Thy will be done in earth, as it is in heaven. Give us this day our daily bread. And forgive us our debts, as we forgive our debtors. And lead us not into temptation, but deliver us from evil: For Thine is the kingdom, and the power, and the glory, forever" (Matt. 6:9–13).

"Ask, and it shall be given you; seek, and ye shall find; knock, and it shall be opened unto you" (Matt. 7:7).

"Beware of false prophets, which come to you in sheep's clothing, but inwardly they are ravening wolves" (Matt. 7:15).

"I send you forth as sheep in the midst of wolves: be ye therefore wise as serpents and harmless as doves" (Matt. 10:16).

"Are not two sparrows sold for a farthing? And one of them shall not fall on the ground without your Father" (Matt. 10:29).

"The Son of Man is Lord even of the Sabbath day" (Matt. 12:8).

"Every kingdom divided against itself is brought to desolation, and every city or house divided against itself shall not stand" (Matt. 12:25).

"Go ye therefore, and teach all nations, baptizing them in the name of the Father, and of the Son, and of the Holy Ghost: Teaching them to observe all things whatsoever I have commanded you: and, lo, I am with you always, even unto the end of the world" (Matt. 28:19–20).

"Render to Caesar the things that are Caesar's, and to God the things that are God's" (Mark 12:17).

"Watch ye and pray, lest ye enter into temptation. The spirit truly is ready, but the flesh is weak" (Mark 14:38).

"If any man will come after Me, let him deny himself, and take up his cross daily, and follow Me" (Luke 9:23).

"It is easier for a camel to go through a needle's eye, than for a rich man to enter into the kingdom of God" (Luke 18:25).

"For the Son of Man is come to seek and to save that which was lost" (Luke 19:10).

"Father, forgive them; for they know not what they do" (Luke 23:34).

"Ye must be born again" (John 3:7).

"I am the bread of life: he that cometh to Me shall never hunger; and he that believeth in Me shall never thirst" (John 6:35).

"If any man thirsts, let him come unto Me, and drink" (John 7:37).

"I am come that they might have life, and that they might have it more abundantly" (John 10:10).

"I am the Good Shepherd: the Good Shepherd giveth his life for the sheep" (John 10:11).

"I and my Father are one" (John 10:30).

"By this shall all men know that ye are My disciples, if ye have love one to another" (John 13:35).

"I am the way, the truth, and the life" (John 14:6).

"Greater love hath no man than this, that a man lay down his life for his friends" (John 15:13).

WHAT DID JESUS SAY ABOUT THE ROMANS?

Jesus' world was part of the Roman Empire. Roman law and Roman soldiers were a part of His everyday life. But

Scripture relates very little of His thoughts concerning them. Nevertheless, His most famous saying about the Romans was in regard to taxation: "Render to Caesar the things that are Caesar's, and to God the things that are God's." Jesus did not regard the Romans as a menace or even a misfortune. Their kingdom was earthly, and His spiritual.

WHAT DID JESUS SAY
ABOUT THE PHARISEES?

Plenty. He warned His disciples to beware of them, to do not as they did but as they said, and to avoid the hypocrisies in which some Pharisees seemed to indulge. One of His most powerful tirades against them appears in Matthew 23:27, "Woe unto you, scribes and Pharisees, hypocrites! for ye are like unto whited sepulchers which indeed appear beautiful outward, but are within full of dead men's bones, and of all uncleanness."

The Pharisees were highly religious (though legalistic) and eagerly awaited the Messiah. They believed themselves to be the very group the Messiah was planning to elevate and employ in His kingdom. But Jesus ran against much that they believed. He didn't keep the Sabbath the same way they did, resisted legalisms, and constantly confronted them about hypocrisies, such as seeking the best seats in the synagogues, making a show when giving money to the poor, praying in public, and wearing a sorrowful face when fasting.

Jesus did say one good thing about the Pharisees—in the Sermon on the Mount: "For I say unto you, that except your righteousness shall exceed the righteousness of the scribes and Pharisees, ye shall in no case enter into the kingdom of heaven" (Matt. 5:20). Jesus recognized that the Pharisees were trying to live righteous lives.

WHAT ARE THE BEATITUDES?

The Beatitudes are eight beautiful statements about the kind of character and righteousness that pleases God, spoken by Jesus in the opening of the Sermon on the Mount (Matt. 5:3–12). Beatitude is a Latin word meaning "blessedness." It derives from the first word of each of Jesus' sayings: "Blessed are...."

WHAT DID JESUS SAY ABOUT FOLLOWING HIM?

Jesus repeatedly told His disciples that they must take up their cross and follow after Him. He seems to have meant that anyone who truly follows Him must be prepared to obey Him to the point of death and beyond.

Matthew 10:16-42 may be the best description of what it means to follow Him. In this passage, He says that He is sending the disciples out as sheep in the midst of wolves. He tells them they'll be delivered up to governors and kings for His sake to give testimony to them. He tells them they may be scourged in the synagogues and hated by many. Still, He assures His followers that they need not fear those who "kill the body, but are not able to kill the soul." They have a legacy in heaven, and nothing can take that away from them.

Perhaps His most somber statement is in Matthew 10:34: "Think not that I am come to send peace on earth: I came not to send peace, but a sword." He goes on to say that mothers and daughters, fathers and sons will be separated because of disagreements about Him. But, He ultimately reassures them that their reward is sure, and whoever so much as gives a cup of cold water to a child will not "lose his reward."

WHY DID JESUS CAST THE MONEY-CHANGERS FROM THE TEMPLE?

Money-changers did a good business in the temple, changing Roman money into "temple money." Worshipers could not buy sacrifices in the temple with normal money because coins had graven images on them. The money-changers took this "pagan" money in exchange for temple money, at a profit.

Jesus was incensed that these merchants had turned God's temple and worship into a business. Thus, He went in (two times—John 2:13–22 and Mark 11:15–18), made a whip of cords, and drove out all the business people, crying, "Make not My Father's house an house of merchandise."

WHAT WAS THE
TRANSFIGURATION?

Jesus took three disciples, Peter, James, and John, and climbed into a mountain wilderness. There on the mountain, Jesus underwent a transformation. In front of the three disciples, He changed in appearance. Matthew says that His face did "shine as the sun" and His garments were "white as the light" (see Matt. 17:1–8). While Jesus stood out before them like this, two Old Testament prophets, Moses and Elijah, appeared with Him, perhaps representing the two major miraculous periods in Hebrew history. They were all bright as the sun and beautiful. While the disciples looked on, a bright cloud came upon them all and a voice from heaven spoke from the cloud. "This is My beloved Son, in whom I am well pleased; hear ye Him." The marvel concluded, and Jesus quieted the disciples alone.

DID JESUS CALL HIMSELF
THE SON OF GOD?

When Jesus revealed He was the Son of God to His disciples, He told them not to tell others. If He proclaimed Himself the Son of God, the high priests and Sadducees would have arrested Him for blasphemy. This would have shortened His ministry.

CHAPTER NINE

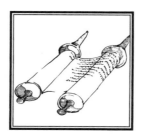

WHAT DOES THE BIBLE SAY ABOUT THE APOSTLES?

WHO WERE JESUS' TWELVE APOSTLES?

Jesus chose twelve disciples to be with Him during His ministry on earth: Simon Peter and his brother Andrew; James and John, the sons of Zebedee; Philip; Bartholomew; Thomas; Matthew, the tax gatherer; James, the son of Alphaeus; Thaddeus; Simon the Zealot; and Judas Iscariot, who betrayed Him.

WHAT HAPPENED TO THE APOSTLES AFTER JESUS DIED?

Judas Iscariot committed suicide. All the others went into the world to spread the news of the Gospel, and all but one were ultimately executed for their efforts. John was exiled to the island of Patmos where some scholars believe he wrote the Book of Revelation. He may have died there or in Ephesus.

WHAT IS THE DIFFERENCE BETWEEN A DISCIPLE AND AN APOSTLE?

"Disciple" means "learner." Rabbis in Jesus' day usually had several disciples who studied with them personally. Jesus gathered twelve disciples who would form His most intimate circle. He also had many other disciples who knew Him and learned from Him but weren't always at His side. Some of these were Mary, Martha, and Lazarus; Mary Magdalene; Cleopas, Salome, and Jesus' mother, Mary.

"Apostle" means "sent one" or "one sent out." The eleven disciples who remained after Jesus' death and resurrection became apostles and were sent out to spread the news of the Gospel. Other apostles were added along the way—Paul, Barnabas, Stephen, John, Mark, Luke, and others. Jesus actually commissioned the twelve disciples as apostles (Matthew 10), but their real ministry as apostles did not begin until after the Holy Spirit came upon them at Pentecost, ten days after Jesus' ascension into heaven (Acts 2).

WHICH APOSTLES
BECAME SAINTS?

All the original apostles are saints in the Roman Catholic Church except Judas Iscariot, for obvious reasons. However, the Bible makes no distinction between a "saint" as simply a believer and the "holy ones" designated later by the church. Peter and John were not selected by Jesus or the Bible for sainthood.

WHERE ARE THE
APOSTLES BURIED?

No one knows where the graves of any of the apostles are. Most were executed and thus probably buried with the poor or with criminals. Some might have been buried in the catacombs around Rome, but no distinct burial places are known.

CHAPTER TEN

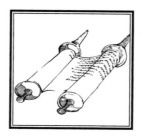

WHAT HOLIDAYS ARE IN THE BIBLE?

WHY DID GOD GIVE ISRAEL FEASTS?

As with all God's legislated laws and special days, the feasts were ways to celebrate religious heritage, to remember great dates in history, and to give the people something to look forward to every season of the year.

WHAT ARE THE GREAT FEASTS OF SCRIPTURE?

In the Old Testament, Leviticus 23, six feasts to the Lord are explained. The sacred year was laid out this way:

Month	Special Day	
Nisan *(April)*	14	Passover
	15	Unleavened bread
	21	Close of Passover
Iyar*(May)*		
Sivan*(June)*	6	Feast of Pentecost
Tammuz *(July)*		
Ab*(August)*		
Elul*(September)*		
Tishri*(October)*	1 & 2	The Feast of Trumpets or Rosh Hashanah
	10	Day of Atonement, or Yom Kippur
	15-21	Feast of Tabernacles
	22	"(Sacred) Assembly"
Marchesvan*(November)*		
Kislev*(December)*	25	Feast of Lights, Hanukkah
Tebeth *(January)*		
Shebet *(February)*		
Adar *(March)*	14	Feast of Purim

Two of these feasts, Lights and Purim, are not mentioned in Leviticus and were not instituted until after the Jews' exile to Babylon.

What were these feasts? Passover was the preeminent feast of Israel. It represented their freedom from slavery in Egypt, and the day the angel of the Lord "passed over" them because of the blood of the lambs placed on their doorsteps and slew the firstborn sons of Egypt, human and animal. Passover in this sense was a "remembrance"—a looking back at what God had done. When Jesus instituted the "Lord's Supper" in the upper room the day before He was crucified, He was celebrating Passover.

The Feast of Pentecost was also called the "Feast of Weeks," or the "Day of First Fruits." It was celebrated 50 days after Passover—thus the word "Pentecost" or "fifty"—on the last day of the wheat harvest. Everyone came to the temple to offer their "first fruits" from the harvest in the form of loaves of leavened bread.

The Feast of Trumpets ushered in the civil year for the Jews with the blowing of trumpets all day. It might be considered comparable to our modern New Year's Day.

The Feast of the Day of Atonement or "Yom Kippur" was the most sacred of all Jewish days. The people fasted and reflected upon the sins of the past year. These were atoned for by sacrifices in the temple.

The Feast of Tabernacles came five days after Yom Kippur. It represented Israel's wandering in the wilderness, and thus Jews traveled to Jerusalem and lived in "booths" made of branches and leaves or in tents around Jerusalem. It marked the last day of all harvests. The "Sacred Assembly" followed the Feast of Tabernacles reminding the people to observe a sacred occasion and bring an offering to the Lord. It is a solemn gathering (Lev. 23:36).

The other two feasts, Lights and Purim, were not instituted until after the exile to Babylon. Purim derives from the
biblical book of Esther. Purim means "lots" and two days
were celebrated as a remembrance of how Queen Esther
saved Israel from extermination. It was a festive occasion.
The whole book of Esther was read aloud in the temple on
these days.

Hanukkah is not mentioned in the Hebrew canon, but is
in the Apocrypha. The Feast of Lights or Hanukkah was
instituted by Judas Maccabeus in 164 B.C. after the temple
had been cleansed and resanctified. It lasted eight days. A
candle on the "menorah" was lit each day until all eight were
glowing on the last day. The great stories of the adventures
of Judas Maccabeus and others were retold to the children.

WHAT IS THE ACTUAL DATE OF CHRISTMAS IN THE BIBLE?

The actual birthday of Jesus is not known. December 25
was instituted by Emperor Constantine after he became a
Christian about A.D. 325. Because different regions of the
world used slightly different calendars, the Eastern
Orthodox church celebrates Christ's birth on January 6, and
the Armenian church on January 19. Over time, various cel-
ebratory traditions became associated with Christ's birth,
such as the giving of presents and the decorating of a tree.
But these came in later years.

IS EASTER MENTIONED IN THE BIBLE?

"Easter" is the term used by the King James Version of the Bible. However, the correct translation is "Passover," Israel's most important feast week. This celebration represented the time in which God spared the Jewish people as He evoked His terrible punishment upon Pharaoh's people by killing first-born sons throughout the land of Egypt (Exod. 5-12).

For Christians, Easter represents resurrection Sunday, the day Jesus rose from the dead. The date was determined by the Council of Nicea in A.D. 325 as "the first Sunday after the full moon following the vernal equinox." Thus, Easter always falls somewhere between March 22 and April 25.

DID PEOPLE IN THE BIBLE CELEBRATE BIRTHDAYS?

One's date of birth has always been an important day and birthday celebrations go back to ancient times. Pharaoh celebrated his "birthday" by giving a feast for all his servants (Gen. 40:20). It was on Herod's birthday (Matt. 14:6) that Salome, the daughter of Herodias, danced for the governor and pleased him so much that he ordered that she be given anything she wanted—which turned out to be John the Baptist's head.

WHAT WAS SERVED—AND CELEBRATED— AT THE LAST SUPPER?

Because this was the Jewish Passover meal, we know precisely what was served: unleavened bread, bitter herbs, wine, and roast lamb. The men lay against pillows around a low table. They used pieces of unleavened bread to scoop up pieces of roast lamb.

Jesus, however, had more to celebrate than the Passover. Jesus knew that this was His "last supper" with His followers. It was at this supper that Jesus instituted the sacrament of the Lord's Supper, which included unleavened bread and wine. According to Paul (1 Cor. 11:23–26), Jesus took the bread and said, "Take, eat: this is My body, which is broken for you: this do in remembrance of Me." He did this at the beginning of the dinner. Then at the end, He took wine and said, "This cup is the new testament in My blood: this do ye, as oft as ye drink it, in remembrance of Me."

The Lord's Supper comes down in tradition as the most important "ordinance" of the Christian faith. It is a remembrance of Christ's death for our sins.

The Roman Catholic Mass is centered around this celebration, which is called the Eucharist, a term that means to show gratitude. Roman Catholic tradition states that the bread and wine actually become the body and blood of Jesus Christ by a mystical process called "transubstantiation."

CHAPTER ELEVEN

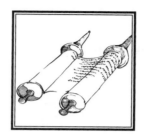

WHAT WAS EVERYDAY LIFE LIKE FOR PEOPLE IN THE BIBLE?

HOW LONG DID PEOPLE LIVE?

Before the Great Flood of Noah, the Old Testament relates that people in antiquity lived far longer than today. Adam lived 930 years. Methuselah lived the longest—969 years. Noah lived 950 years.

After the Great Flood, a person's life span fell into a more familiar range. The Bible says Abraham lived 175 years, Moses died at 120, and Psalms 90:10 said that a man's life contained seventy years, or in cases of great strength, eighty years. This was considered a lengthy and good life in Jesus' day. Jesus was less than forty years old when He was crucified.

WHAT LANGUAGE
DID THEY SPEAK?

In Old Testament times, Hebrew was the dominant language of Jews. Most of the Old Testament is written in Hebrew. However, after the various exiles of the Israelite people, the Assyrian diplomatic tongue of Aramaic became most common. The exiles returning about 536 B.C. probably spoke Aramaic or a mixture of several Hebrew dialects.

In Jesus' day, Aramaic and Koine (common) Greek were the usual languages spoken by the people. Presumably, Jesus spoke both Aramaic and Greek and could also read and speak biblical Hebrew. He may even have known Latin, the language of the Romans.

The apostles all wrote in Koine Greek, so they must have spoken it fluently. Paul, a learned man who studied with some of the great rabbis of Israel, must also have spoken Aramaic and Hebrew.

COULD PEOPLE READ
AND WRITE?

Reading and writing were common, though not everyone was literate. Jews were careful to educate their children in the faith, and many had personal tutors to instruct their children. Most instruction in the days following Abraham occurred in the home. Fathers and mothers were strictly commanded to teach their children all the rudiments and regulations of their faith (Deut. 6:4–9). As early as the time of Moses, people were instructed to write the law on their door posts.

After the Babylonian exile ended about the fifth century B.C., synagogues became the local places for worship, instruction, and schooling. Normally, a teacher might have twenty-five students, and he would teach reading, writing, and arithmetic, using the Old Testament as the primary text. By the time of Jesus, schools, traveling tutors, rabbis, and other means of education were common. Obviously, Jesus knew how to read and write. Memorization and drills were the primary forms of learning.

Jesus' disciples could probably read and write, though some were rough fishermen. But it's possible that Peter couldn't, and had someone transcribe his words.

WHAT PROFESSIONS
EXISTED IN BIBLICAL TIMES?

The culture of Abraham and those following him was largely agricultural. They had herds of sheep, cattle, donkeys, camels, and goats that were nurtured and watched, and others farmed with the help of slaves and paid laborers. After Abraham's time, the Jewish tribes were nomadic, living in tents, and moving with the seasons and richness of land.

As the people of Israel moved closer to nationhood, various other kinds of work came to the fore: fishing, merchandizing, weaving, engraving, trade, soldiering, blacksmithing, iron working, horse trading and training, teaching and preaching, seafaring, and a multitude of other kinds of work. The Jewish culture was a lively culture, with many people specializing in many professions. As carpenters, Jesus and His father must have had a carpentry shop as a means of commissioning various jobs.

Men usually took their fathers' professions. The home and the trade of the father were passed down to the sons in an orderly and complete fashion. Family secrets were passed along as well. A family's recipe for bread or a particular way of handling the making of a chair were formalized so that certain families became well-known for their skills.

HOW WERE THEY PAID?

Before money was coined and printed, many people bartered in goods. A family's wealth was in their farms, livestock, household furnishings, garments, and metals. Gold, silver, and copper were traded by weight and quality before they began to be formed into coins. Thus, a trader would weigh and calculate the value of whatever he wanted to trade. Originally, the shekel was a unit of weight.

Gradually, though, coins began to be minted and became the standard currency. The early Egyptians and Hittites made rings and rounded nodules of gold, silver, and copper as a way of standardizing the exchange.

The first mention we have of actual coins in the Bible is in Ezra 8:27, which refers to twenty basins worth 1,000 drams (or darics). The daric was a Persian gold coin that got its name from Darius I (521–486 B.C.). It's believed that the kings of Lydia were the first people to make coins in the sixth or seventh century B.C. After 138 B.C., the Maccabeans made the first Hebrew coins. These had a chalice on the face and a three-branched pomegranate on the back.

In New Testament times, the Roman denarius, a silver coin with a picture of Caesar on the face, was the most widely known. The Greek equivalent was the drachma. Most money was made of silver. However, when the widow gave the "mites" to the Temple treasury (which Jesus praised as worth more than anything the rich people gave), she was giving a coin called a lepta, worth about one-sixteenth of a denarius (Mark 12:41–44).

On another occasion, a temple tax collector asked Jesus whether He had paid the two-drachma tax. In order to comply, Jesus sent people to catch a fish, in the mouth of which was found a stater, a coin worth four drachma (Matt. 17:24–27).

There were other coins in Roman times, but no others mentioned in Scripture.

WHAT WAS THE AVERAGE INCOME OF A WORKER?

The average pay of a laborer or a soldier was one denarius a day. In silver value, that was about the equivalent of a modern quarter. Thus, the income for a year would be about 365 denarii. In modern terms, this would be the equivalent of $40-$50 a day, or about $18,000 dollars a year. However, this is a very inexact comparison.

WHAT DID BIBLICAL PEOPLE GROW AND EAT?

Grapes, wheat, barley, fitches (nutmeg flowers), and emmer, a kind of wheat, were common, as were spelt, millet, and rye. The last three were coarse grains cultivated on the edges of fields and used in making bread. Other crops were flagon, pomegranate, melons, and a lemon-like fruit called a citron. Cultivated agricultural products included dates, figs, flax to make linen cloth, lentils, coarse beans, chick peas, cucumbers, onions, leeks, garlic, almonds, and pistachios. All these required careful attention and were grown all over the Holy Land.

People drank milk from cows, goats, and camels, as well as water, wine, and fruit juice.

Jewish law allowed people to eat all fish with fins and scales such as those caught in the Mediterranean and the sea of Galilee. These people also ate calf, kid, sheep, and lamb. However, their primary diet was fruits and vegetables, and they ate meat mainly on festival occasions.

COULD FOOD BE PRESERVED?

Food was generally eaten soon after it had been prepared. Bread was baked daily so that it was ready for the evening meal or supper. While fish could be broiled and preserved as a salty, thin kind of jerky, and drying meats was also possible, though not ordinary, people ate mostly fresh fruits and vegetables. Meat was slaughtered the day it was eaten, as Abraham did when the angel of the Lord visited him (Genesis 18) and as the fatted calf was slain in the story of the Prodigal Son (Luke 15). Of course, the wealthy dug root cellars that provided cool storage for perishables, which helped extend the life of some foods.

The marketplace has been a longstanding tradition of many peoples. Before preservation methods were widely used, people visited the marketplace nearly every day. The "milkman" might come to the market with his milk freshly drawn that morning. Butchers displayed their freshly butchered meats, farmers their produce, and artisans their pots, pottery, knives, and metal implements. The marketplace was a social and economic gathering center for the people. It was a place to meet with members of the community and buy, sell, gossip, preach (Paul often visited the marketplace as a first venue for evangelism), and be entertained.

HOW DID THEY COOK?

Hearths are mentioned in the Bible as early as Abraham's day. He told Sarah on one occasion to bake bread on the hearth (Gen. 18:6). This was probably not an enclosed oven, but stones laid on top of the fire, on which when heated, bread could be baked.

Meat was simmered in a cauldron and dipped out with a three-pronged fork or, more common in later times, roasted in an oven. Frequently, meat was broiled right over a fire in the same way that we cook meat on a grill today. Vegetables were boiled or roasted. Fruits were served fresh.

WHAT WAS A TYPICAL MEAL?

Typically two daily meals were eaten—one in the morning, a light breakfast, of milk, bread, fruit, and cheese, normally between nine o'clock and noon. The evening meal came after the heat of the day died down, at seven or eight o'clock in summer. Meat, fish, butter and bread, fruits, vegetables, and wine were usually served, though meat was rare except among the rich and well-to-do.

In ancient times there was no dining table. People gathered around a circular skin on which the food sat. A bowl with meat and broth stood in the middle. Diners took pieces of bread (there were no utensils), called "sops," and dipped them into the stew, taking out pieces of meat or cooked vegetable. This was how Jesus and His disciples ate in the Upper Room, when Jesus dipped His sop into the lamb stew and gave it to Judas Iscariot, as a sign of respect.

Tables had become common by the time of Jesus. They were raised slightly above the level of the floor. Diners sat on couches, with their legs stretched out away from the table and their heads close to the bowls. People leaned their left elbows on the table and ate with their right hands, dipping the sop into the broth and meat. At the Last Supper, John could easily have reclined, bent back, and laid his head on Jesus' chest (John 13:21-26).

Various kinds of pots and bowls of clay were used all through the ancient world, as were metal pots and cauldrons. King Solomon's temple was famous for its gold and silver pots and plates used in temple worship.

WHAT CLOTHING DID BIBLICAL PEOPLE WEAR?
Since ancient times, men and women have known how to weave and use different kinds of materials for creating

clothing of all sorts. They learned to spin and weave wool, hair, cotton, flax, and eventually Chinese silk.

Among biblical people, clothing indicated not only a person's class, trade, or profession, but also gave a ceremonial formality to specific occasions. For instance, people had clothing that would only be worn at festivals and feasts. This finery was colorful, lavish, and sumptuous. The primary colors worn were purple, scarlet, yellow, blue, and black; white was the most special, representing purity, confidence, and joy. Kings and royalty wore purple on special occasions, but white remained the top preference. Paul's convert in Philippi, Lydia, was a businesswoman and a dealer in "purple." She sold dyes and possibly garments that had been dyed purple (Acts 16).

For men in biblical times, daily clothing included an inner tunic, the tunic coat, the girdle, the cloak, headdress, and sandals or shoes. The inner tunic, made of cotton or linen, extended to the loins like a long shirt and was worn next to the skin. When the weather was hot, it might not be worn at all.

The tunic coat was a man's public clothing. It was close-fitting, like a shirt, and extended to the knees or ankles. Sometimes tunics were of one color, but more often were many, striped in green, blue, yellow, black, white, and red.

The girdle was a leather belt or cloth sash folded over to form a pouch, which could carry personal items or food. The girdle held the tunic in place.

The outer cloak or mantle came in two styles—the "me-il" and the "simlah." The me-il was a long, loose-fitting cloak which covered all the above garments. It was normally worn by priests, politicians, and men in the professions. It might have been the "coat of many colors" that Jacob gave to Joseph and that so infuriated his brothers. It was a cloak of distinction, authority, and privilege. It was frequently made of cotton, linen, or silk, and embroidered on the edges, or edged with fur.

The simlah was the lower-class version—simpler and made of camel hair, wool, or goat hair. It was rough, and the owner would wrap himself in it to sleep at night. When a lawsuit was pending, the plaintiff could not keep a man's outer cloak longer than the end of the day; it was all he had to keep warm at night.

For headwear, men wore caps, turbans, or head-scarves. The cap, like a small skullcap, was normally worn by the lower classes. The turban, wound around the head so that the ends were concealed, was the dress of the rich and privileged. The head-scarf was also common. Made of a square yard of cloth, usually of linen or wool, it was folded into a triangle and draped around the head. All these forms of headwear protected against the sun.

Women's wear had, by Jewish law, to be different from men's. Though some articles were similar, the way women's garments were cut and embroidered and colored easily distinguished them from men's. Women's garments always reached to the feet for modesty and propriety. Their headdresses also differed from men's. A wealthy woman might pin her headdress to a small cap made of pearls or jewels. A married woman usually wore coins on her headdress, jangling and dangling, to represent her dowry. The undergarments were of silk, cotton, or linen, depending on the woman's class and station in life. Over this was the undershirt with long sleeves. It extended to the knees. Over the undershirt was a tightly fitting jacket, sometimes called a petticoat, which was often beautiful in appearance, scarlet in color, and with fine embroidery all around the edges. We do not know precisely how women wore veils in those days. Sometimes there were double veils, of one kind of cloth for below the nose and another for the eyes and above.

In the ancient world, a woman's hair was extremely valued, and she often showed it to advantage plaited and arranged in fashionable ways. Women adorned themselves with jewelry including bracelets, earrings, and nose rings.

WHAT MATERIALS WERE USED TO MAKE CLOTHING?

Undergarments were woven from wool, cotton, flax, and silk. Outer garments were made of goat's hair, camel's hair, and wool. Clothing was made very much as it is today. Wool, flax, cotton, and other fibers were spun; women spun hairs into threads that could be woven into lengths of cloth. The Bible says Jesus' robe, which the Romans gambled for as He hung on the cross, was seamless—of one weave and not stitched together. It was very expensive, and clearly the Romans who gambled for it weren't willing to simply give it away.

As in any open market, costs varied from very inexpensive for the poor to exceedingly costly for the rich. What determined the price was the material used and the quality of craftsmanship. As is true today, clothing made by a noted tradesman or tailor could command much higher prices.

Just how costly these garments were is hinted at in the Scripture. Joshua 7 relates the tale of Achan, who during the destruction of Jericho, found a "goodly Babylonish garment" that he knew was costly by its beauty and work. Although such things were under the "ban" of God and couldn't be kept, he stole it and hid it in his tent. His family paid a high price for his deceit—they were all stoned, women and children included, because they had complicity in the crime.

Jesus also shed light on the value of dress when He said, "Lay not up for yourselves treasure upon earth, where moth and rust doth corrupt, and where thieves break through and steal. . ." (Matt. 6:19). When Jesus mentioned "moth," He was referring to the practice of storing up wealth in the form of garments. A person's wealth in those days had three forms: gold and silver, goods such as quantities of wheat (like the "rich fool" of the parable), and clothing. Jesus said that none of it was secure, so we shouldn't invest our money and lives in such things. Nevertheless, people considered their wardrobe a form of wealth.

At night, homeless people or travelers would wrap themselves in their cloaks and sleep on pallets in the night air, in a cave, or in a rough shelter. He or she would normally wear the undergarment or tunic close to the body, but the cloak would provide the warmth of a blanket.

Rich people, of course, had more elaborate bed quarters, with a bedstead, runners, and a headboard. The pallet that was on the bed was stuffed with feathers, wool, or some other soft material. The pillow was made of linen or silk. Poor people had pillows made of goat's skin.

WHAT DID SOLDIERS WEAR?

Paul provides a fairly apt picture of a soldier's spiritual dress in Ephesians 6:11–18. Normally, a soldier wore a breastplate made of hard leather, metal, or even gold in the case of Roman generals in dress uniform. It was tied in the back by leather thongs and protected the chest and vital organs.

Underneath the breastplate, the tunic reached almost to the knees. Around the waist stretched the girdle (which Paul calls the "girdle of truth"), which held the whole outfit together. Shin guards covered the legs below the knee. Sandals, fashioned with rough and hard treads, gave the soldier secure footing while fighting. The soldier carried a shield and wore a helmet on his head. Among the Hebrews, every man over the age of twenty served time as a soldier and they formed regiments by tribes.

DID BIBLICAL PEOPLE TRAVEL?

Yes. The Bible gives many examples of long and arduous trips. Abraham traveled from Ur to Haran to Canaan on the authority of God's covenant. That was a journey of well over a thousand miles. Jacob, a generation later, made the journey from Canaan to Haran, where he found his wives, Leah and Rachel, and served Laban until he had become rich. After returning to Canaan, Jacob's sons traveled to Egypt in search of wheat and food. After Joseph revealed himself to them, the whole family journeyed to Egypt, again a journey of more than 500 miles. The people of Israel wandered in the desert of the Sinai Peninsula for forty years. Elijah outran King Ahab from Mt. Carmel to the king's palace at Jezreel, a journey of forty miles. Joseph and Mary journeyed from Galilee to Bethlehem while Mary was pregnant, a journey by donkey of nearly eighty miles. Obviously, travel in the times when roads, inns, and police were rare was hazardous but unavoidable.

For safety, people commonly traveled in a group or caravan. Mary and Joseph traveled in a caravan from Jerusalem back to Galilee, the time Jesus left them to talk with the rabbis in the temple. Donkeys and carts were common. Donkeys in particular were excellent for travel in the desert because, unlike camels, they could eat the thin coarse grasses found there.

People domesticated the camel more than 4,000 years ago—and because of its endurance and ability to traverse arid landscapes, it was called the "ship of the desert." A camel could pull a plow or carry a load, and it could transport a load of 500 pounds over 100 miles a day.

Horses were rarer than donkeys and camels, owing to their richer dietary needs. King Solomon raised an army of horses and his stables have been excavated in Jerusalem. However, horses did not naturally flourish in the desert climate, as donkeys and camels did.

Chariots were one means of shorter travel through the Roman world and Egypt, especially for armies. But chariots were far too expensive for common people. The Ethiopian eunuch was traveling by chariot when Philip was carried up by the Spirit and set down nearby (Acts 8).

At first, roads were little more than sheep and cattle trails through fields. But as caravan routes became more common, roads began to be established. Some roads followed wadis, the beds of streams and rivers that were formed in flood season. Eventually, travel routes pushed through mountain passes, joining together existing roads. Canaan was at the crossroads of most trade and caravan routes.

The Via Maris, one of the most famous trade routes, cut across Canaan following the coastline of the Mediterranean into Egypt.

Another great road was King's Highway. It ran east and west from Damascus to Saudi Arabia. It was much rougher than the Via Maris but was also a well-traveled, profitable trade route.

The Pax Romana, or Roman peace, was established by Rome as it conquered most of the known world. While this limited the freedom of a nation and people, it opened both economic and cultural ties throughout the empire and generated hundreds of years of peace and tranquility.

Travelers did not need permission to move about, but letters from authorities could promise easier passage and cooperation from the locals.

Many of the earliest travelers employed guides and scouts to lead them on journeys and to provide knowledge of oases and outposts on the trade routes that offered water, food, baths, and so on.

At the height of their power, the Romans were the greatest road makers in the world. In over five centuries they built 50,000 miles of high-quality roads and 320,000 miles of back roads. The Romans built these roads to last. They were constructed in several layers. The foundation roadbed was constructed of packed-down gravel and rocks. On top of that they spread a layer of concrete very similar to modern concrete. Finally, on top of the concrete, the Romans placed large stones—twelve inches deep and as much as eighteen inches wide, all fitted together so that the surface was relatively smooth. Road width ranged from twenty feet in the much-used suburban areas and cities to six feet on the mountains. The Appian Way, the primary road from Rome extending over 360 miles to Brundisium on the Adriatic Sea, was begun in 312 B.C. and was eighteen feet wide in most places. The Romans were excellent surveyors and carefully mapped the progress of their road building so that the authorities in Rome could readily see what was happening. Many Roman roads still exist today.

Traveling by sea was also common. The great shipping prowess of the Phoenicians and the lure of trading with far and distant peoples helped to expand the world of biblical people. Ships were largely powered by sail. Galleys were oar-driven military boats such as the one in which Jonah fled for Tarshish. The preponderance of these two types of boats made water transportation common and cheap. They were the fastest means of traveling from Canaan to Italy and other distant destinations where natural barriers prevented easy access by land.

WHAT KIND OF SHIPS
WERE USED?

The ships of yesteryear were small, cramped, dangerous, and smelly. They were not for the delicate or the pleasure-seeker. In fact, few ship travelers were tourists; ships were for either trade or defense.

From earliest times, sailors harnessed the winds to travel the seas. They constructed ships from great cedar and oak trees from the forests of Canaan and Lebanon, making the masts from cedar, the oars of oak. Just like today, a ship was guided by a rudder and powered by sail. The trade routes stretched from Phoenicia to Tarshish, Italy, Egypt, and all the Mediterranean countries. The Egyptians succeeded with the massive endeavor of building a canal from the Mediterranean to the Red Sea. In 1980–1935 B.C., which many people believe was the time Abraham lived, Pharaoh Sesostris used a branch of the Nile to fashion a canal from the Nile at modern Zagazig through the land of Goshen all the way to Lake Timsah. At that point it turned south, through the Bitter Lakes, and continued on into the Red Sea. But over time the relentlessly hostile elements of sun, heat, and sandstorms destroyed this canal and its successors.

WHAT RELIGIONS DID PEOPLE IN THE BIBLE PRACTICE?

In the Old Testament, idolatry, Baal worship, and other cults were prevalent, and continual problems arose between God and the Jews. God punished the Jews frequently for their interest in idols and their practice of the forbidden traditions, which included religious prostitution and child sacrifice. The term Baal has different meanings: lord, possessor, husband. But in Israel it largely represented the head over the gods of a certain locale. The Canaanites, who lived in the land of Israel before Israel conquered it under Joshua, worshiped Baal. Their influence was greatly felt and soon many Israelites dabbled in this worship, too. A tremendous conflict arose between Jehovah and Baal that ultimately led to God punishing Israel for their "adultery" and sending the Israelites into slavery.

Judaism was obviously the religion of the Jews during the days of Jesus. In fact, most of Jesus' conflicts were with the religious leaders who in some ways had taken Judaism too far. Pharisees, the primary protectors of the Jewish faith in Jesus' day, were one of the most prominently orthodox sects, and they vigorously defended the Sabbath, the law, and the tenets of their beliefs.

Within Israel there was a special sect called "Nazirites." Their regulations and laws are found in Numbers 6. These were men and women who were specially dedicated to the service of the Lord. They could not use a razor, drink wine (or even eat grapes), or touch a dead body. Some famous

Nazirites found in the Bible are Samson (the reason for his long hair), Samuel, and John the Baptist.

The Sadducees, another Jewish sect composed of the elite and aristocratic members of society, did not believe in the resurrection or angels and only recognized the first five books of Moses as the authoritative Bible. They did not recognize the prophets.

There were also the Zealots, Jews committed to overthrowing the Romans. Among them were assassins, saboteurs, and others who would do anything in the name of faith to throw off the yolk of Rome's domination.

Finally, there were the Essenes, believed by many to be the cult that hid the Dead Sea Scrolls in caves. This group was a sect of Judaism, whose members generally did not marry and were ascetic and rigorous in their practice of religion. Not much is known about them, and they are not mentioned in the Bible.

There were, of course, other religions practiced in the days of Jesus. The Samaritans had their own special practices that were decidedly Jewish in custom, but mixed with other religions they had adapted in their exile. Thus, the woman at the well in John 4 talked to Jesus about the fact that Samaritans and Jews differed about where to worship God. Samaritans worshiped at Gerizim im Samaria; Jews worshiped at Jerusalem. The Romans had many "mystery" religions, mysterious in the sense that they included many secret arts and hidden practices. Caesar worship, and the worship of the gods of their pantheon (Jupiter, Mercury, and so on), which corresponded to the gods of Greek mythology. However, none of these were prominent in the Middle East during New Testament times.

WHERE DID PEOPLE IN THE BIBLE WORSHIP?

Throughout Israel's history, various places were established for worship. Each of the patriarchs—Abraham, Isaac, and Jacob—worshiped God at times by simply building an altar of rocks in the wilderness and bowing in prayer, or offering a sacrifice. Later, Moses instituted the Law and worship in the tabernacle, literally a large tent. This was the practice of Israel from the beginning until the time of King Solomon, who built the first temple.

In idol-worshiping cultures, many gods required appeasement at different times of the year. Cities like Corinth were full of temples to various gods, and Athens had so many that they even had a temple to "the unknown god," which Paul used as a step-off point for proclaiming the Gospel. All the people worshiped at temples, from the youngest children to the aged.

The first Christians gathered in the main temple at Jerusalem, in synagogues, and in private homes. In Acts 19:9, Paul mentions that some Christians were meeting at the school of Tyrannus, which indicates that they might have rented a facility. There is no evidence that Christians actually constructed their own churches in the first century after the resurrection of Christ. When the persecutions began, Christians met in secret places, such as the catacombs of Rome. They used a secret symbol, the picture of the fish, to indicate a place where Christians could find solace, help, and fellowship. The fish symbol was used because the Greek word for "fish"—Ichthus—was an acronym for the names of Jesus. The first letters of "Jesus Christ, Son of God, Savior" spelled Ichthus in Greek.

Christians first met on Sunday evenings, the first day of the week and the day on which Jesus rose from the dead. Before long they began meeting on Sunday mornings and evenings to accommodate those who had to work. They did this mostly in secret, because the persecutions had begun with the reign of Nero in A.D. 64.

New Testament teaching, though, instructs us that "whenever two or three are gathered in the name of Christ," there He is also (Matt.18:18-20).

HOW DID THEY CHOOSE RELIGIOUS LEADERS?

Under the Law in the Old Testament, priests were selected from the tribe of Levi. The entire tribe was dedicated to the priestly work and class. Priests worked in the tabernacle (and later the Temple) and carried out the necessary sacrifices for the people. People came to the temple, confessed their sins and procured a sheep, goat, bull, or dove (depending upon their station in society) for sacrifice.

Priests in Israel were different from rabbis. Rabbi means "master" and in the time of Jesus, anyone could become a teacher, so long as he was called by God and had spiritual gifts. Priests had to be descendants of Levi.

The early church emphasized the use of the spiritual gifts within its congregation. As early as Paul's first letters, it's clear that the mature members of churches appointed elders and deacons for the work of ministry (Acts 6). Not long after Jesus' resurrection, the church in Jerusalem appointed seven deacons to serve tables at their love feasts. Later, church leaders took on various responsibilities. Paul wrote to the Ephesians that God gave "some apostles; and some, prophets; and some, evangelists; and some, pastors and teachers; for the perfecting of the saints. . ." (Eph. 4:11–12). Paul makes clear in 1 Corinthians 12:28, that the highest office in the church was first apostles, secondarily prophets, and thirdly teachers. The apostles and prophets laid the foundation of the church, and others built upon that foundation. All these others were considered ministers.

DID PEOPLE TITHE?

Paying tribute to rulers and as a religious duty has been common from ancient times. It was done in Babylonia, Assyria, Egypt, and even China. By the time Abraham offered to Melchizedek as a tithe all the spoils from the destruction of the kings who took Lot and his family (see Gen. 14), it's obvious he understood the tradition. When Jacob made a covenant with God at Beth-el, he decided to pay tithes (Gen. 28). By law, Israelites were required to pay tithes to Levites, the priestly class in Israel (Deut. 14:22–26). Tithe means a "tenth," and it meant that a person gave a tenth of his flocks, produce, and wealth to the temple and the system that followed.

After the exile, when the people of Israel returned to Judea to rebuild the Temple and the walls of Jerusalem, conflict about tithing was discussed by the prophet Malachi. He told the people in the name of God, "Bring ye all the tithes into the storehouse, that there may be meat in Mine house, and prove Me now herewith, . . . if I will not open you the windows of heaven, and pour you out a blessing that there shall not be room enough to receive it" (Mal. 3:10). Tithing by then was considered a normal part of religious life and essential to one's prosperity.

In the New Testament, tithing as such is not taught. Paul told the Corinthians, "Upon the first day of the week let every one of you lay by him in store, as God hath prospered him, that there be no gatherings when I come" (1 Cor. 16:2). Thus, giving to the church was as a person prospered. In some cases a tenth might be appropriate, for others, less than a tenth might be adequate, while for still others a greater portion should be given. The point is that God wanted us to give as we prospered, not just automatically offer a fixed percentage. This insured that everyone would give as best they could.

HOW OFTEN WERE RELIGIOUS SERVICES HELD?

For the people of Israel, the Sabbath was sacred. This was the seventh day of the week, and it began at sundown on Friday night and went to sundown on Saturday night. No work was to be done. The people worshiped God in the temple at first, and later in the synagogues by readings of the word of God and exposition by a teacher.

The early Christians met on the first day of the week, Sunday, to commemorate the resurrection of Christ. Initially, the Old Testament Scriptures were read and explained by someone learned in the faith. Later, Paul's letters and other documents also became available to read. The elders presided, and the church gathered primarily to celebrate the Lord's Supper. Sometimes they did this as part of the evening meal and had a Love Feast, which began with breaking bread and concluded with drinking wine.

WHAT ARE MARTYRS?

"Martyr" in Greek means "witness." We read in the Bible that under the persecutions of various monarchs and rulers, beginning with the stoning of Stephen (see Acts 7), martyrs came to be known as ones who gave final witness to their faith signed in blood. Jesus said in Matthew 10:17–20, "But beware of men: for they will deliver you up to the councils, and they will scourge you in their synagogues; and ye shall be brought before governors and kings for My sake, for a testimony against them and the Gentiles. But when they deliver you up, take no thought how or what ye shall speak; for it shall be given you in that same hour what ye shall speak. For it is not ye that speak, but the Spirit of your Father which speaketh in you."

It was because of this act of "witnessing," speaking in the Spirit for the name of Christ to the persecutors, that they came to be known as martyrs.

Foxe's *Book of Martyrs* describes many martyrs who gave testimony to their faith before dying. They obviously served God by telling of His glory and goodness even at the moment they were put to death. Stephen preached to his listeners, among whom was Saul (who became Paul), as they threatened him. But when he spoke of the previous persecution of prophets by some Jews and how they did not keep the law, the incensed crowd stoned him. As the stones flew and he lay dying, he prayed, "Lord, lay not this sin to their charge" (Acts 7:60). It was similar to the prayer Jesus uttered when He was nailed to the cross: "Father, forgive them; for they know not what they do" (Luke 23:34).

CHAPTER TWELVE

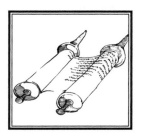

WHAT WERE FAMILIES LIKE IN THE BIBLE?

WHAT DO WE KNOW ABOUT FAMILIES IN THE BIBLE?

In the ancient world, the family was truly extended. It included parents, children, grandparents, grandchildren, and great-grandparents. If families didn't live in the same house, they usually lived in the same vicinity. Families could include as many as seventy or more members, as Jacob's did when he went to Egypt to live in Goshen. While some families were childless, or consisted of only a few members, Hebrews regarded large families as the norm. A family was not only bound by kin, culture, and religion, but shared economic wealth and knowledge.

In early times, many families lived a nomadic lifestyle, moving with the seasons or as lands became barren to more fertile areas to provide the best fields for their animals. Families kept their livestock, property, farms, skills, and businesses within the family, so that many generations might labor and build upon a single enterprise. Men and women worked well into their old age, alongside the younger generations. Jesus learned carpentry from His father, and it is plain from records and historians that this was the normal practice.

Beyond the extended family, though, was a grouping known as the clan. This could include hundreds of men and women, all related by blood to some common ancestor. Normally, a clan had a leader called a "goel" or "kinsman-redeemer." This person was usually well-to-do, and he was required to preserve the clan as best he could against divisiveness or disintegration. This meant that if one of the clan members wanted to sell a piece of land outside the clan, the goel was given the opportunity to purchase the land for the clan first. If a man sold himself into slavery, the goel was to try to buy him back to keep the clan together. The Book of Ruth is a good example of this process. One of the rights of the goel was to marry a recent widow. The widow Ruth worked in the fields of Boaz, but while Boaz wished to claim her for his own wife, she had to be offered to the goel first. Because the goel was willing to forego his obligations, the two were permitted to marry.

As is true now, families found in the Bible suffered their ups and downs, too. Beginning with Cain and Abel, the Bible relates countless stories of greed, jealousy, lust, and murder between family members. Esau and Jacob were bitter rivals for their parents' affections. Jacob's own sons sold their brother Joseph into slavery. Intermarriage, even between a brother and sister, was not unknown. Although it was prohibited, the friends of a lovesick Amnon, King David's son, counseled him to ask his father for his half sister Tamar's hand in marriage. But the Bible relates that he instead raped her, bringing carnage and ill consequences into the family.

WHERE DID FAMILIES LIVE?

Until the establishment of cities after the Israelites reclaimed the promised land, the Hebrews lived largely in tents. A tent was made of skins or cloth stretched over poles and held down by stakes, much as tents are today. A doorway provided the way into the tent. The fire was usually kindled in the center and the smoke escaped through a hole in the roof. Sometimes people used curtains to divide tents into rooms. When Israel conquered the land of Canaan, they claimed the abandoned houses. Many of these houses were made of clay bricks, sun- or furnace-dried and mortared with clay, mud, or pitch. The houses had one central room where all the daily chores were performed. A hole in the roof provided a skylight and also a way for smoke to escape the cooking fire. Windows might be cut into the walls high up to let light in. Bed mats lay in corners on the dirt or stone-packed floor.

Outside the house was a fenced yard for the animals. A stairway to the top of the house provided a place to sleep on the roof, which was thatched or made of stone lying on beams. The children often slept on the roof to provide privacy for their parents at night.

HOW DID THE RICH LIVE?

In the cities, the rich had large, lavish houses that would appear opulent even by modern standards. Ordinarily, the house was built around an open rectangular court, which might have had a well in the middle. Around the court, various rooms were arranged for different purposes—the kitchen, the master's quarters, and so on. The master's quarters featured fine wooden furniture made by the best craftsmen. Figurines and possibly an idol would be found along the sides of the room. On three sides there might be long couches on which visitors could sit and which also doubled as beds. The wife's and daughter's rooms might be upstairs, and only the master was allowed to visit these rooms.

Also on the ground floor were the kitchen, rooms for storing food, and the slaves' quarters. These were quite plain.

On the second floor the spacious rooms, mostly bedrooms, doubled as meeting rooms. Paul once preached a sermon in one of these rooms that lasted so long that one of the men, Eutychus, fell asleep and dropped to the floor as if dead. Paul revived him, then went on preaching (Acts 20).

Another room common to the houses of the rich was the alliyeh, a room built over the porch and extending into the street. This room was often used to store clothing or other items and to provide a small retreat for meditation, reading, or relaxation. Jesus probably referred to this room when He told us to go into our closets to pray (Matt. 6).

The roofs on the houses were made of a kind of cement that dried and cracked in the sun. Often, to keep the rain out, a house owner would lay patches of grass on the roof over the cracked surfaces. A roof might also be made of clay tiles or flat stones.

There were windows along the sides and front of the houses. They were closed by lattices and shutters. There was no glass in Hebrew windows because glass was relatively unknown. Doors did not have hinges, but rather, at their tops and bottoms had circular shafts that projected into holes in the upper and lower door frames.

The houses of the rich were built with fine materials: stone and brick outside walls, marble and cedar interior walls. Haggai railed against the Jews after the exile because they dwelled in "cedar houses" while God's house lay in ruins.

WHEN WERE CHILDREN CONSIDERED ADULTS?

The "age of accountability" was normally considered to be twenty years old, although sons might be considered adult at age thirteen, the same age at which today's Jewish boys and girls are no longer considered children.

WHAT WAS MARRIAGE LIKE?

A woman was betrothed to her husband when an agreement was reached between her family and the groom's. Usually marriages were arranged by families and were not the love matches we have today. Once a prospect was found, the father and groom negotiated a bride-price, which the groom would give to the father in exchange for his bride. The betrothal period before the actual marriage was usually about one year. However, when a couple was betrothed, they were considered married, and a legal divorce would be necessary to dissolve the agreement. Thus, Joseph, when he found out Mary was pregnant, "desired to put her away secretly"—to divorce her—(Matt. 1). However, an angel appeared to him in a dream and assured him that Mary had not committed adultery. Joseph formalized the marriage and took her to Bethlehem. He did not consummate their union until after Jesus was born.

HOW WERE WEDDINGS CELEBRATED?

The Old Testament frequently describes wedding celebrations lasting as long as a week. The two families provided the festivities, and much of their honor among their people was perceived by how well they served guests at a wedding. At Cana, when Jesus and His disciples attended a marriage, the hosts ran out of wine. This was considered a major social offense, and it became necessary for them to do something to preserve their honor. Jesus turned the water into wine to save the hosts' reputations.

Wedding ceremonies may have been performed by religious leaders. But sometimes the bond was made much simpler by a simple public statement or act. This was shown in the story of Isaac and Rebekah in Genesis 24:67 where "Isaac brought her into his mother Sarah's tent and took Rebekah, and she became his wife; and he loved her."

Presents were often given by the groom's family to the bride and vice-versa. Caleb gave Othniel and his daughter Achsah the lavish gifts of a field and the springs of water. The Egyptian Pharaoh gave Solomon the city of Gezer as a wedding present.

A bride from a wealthy family could adorn herself in a special wedding dress which was laden with riches such as pearls and coins, but it was the groom who was the center of attention on his wedding day and whose joy was the primary concern. Both the bride and groom had attendants who accompanied them to the wedding and joined in the revelry.

WHY DID SOME MEN IN THE BIBLE HAVE MANY WIVES OR CONCUBINES?

In the early years, a man sometimes married a second wife or arranged for a concubine because his first wife was barren. Abraham and Jacob both chose this complex marital responsibility when Abraham slept with Hagar, and Jacob had children with the handmaids of his two wives, Leah and Rachel. Sometimes, though, a daughter would be offered in marriage by a ruler as the means of establishing an alliance between families or countries that would ensure a lasting peace or significant financial gain.

Some men of wealth and power took more than one wife or concubine for other reasons. We know that King David had at least ten concubines and probably more. Other people in scripture who had concubines were Eliphaz, Gideon, King Saul, Caleb, Manasseh, Rehoboam, Abijah, and Belshazzar. Scripture states that Solomon topped the list—with 700 wives and 300 concubines. While the Old Testament does not forbid having more than one wife, having excessive numbers of wives is still discouraged (Deut. 17:14-17).

A concubine was not just a man's lover but a woman joined to him by law. However, she did not have all the privileges and power of the wife or wives with whom the man was joined in marriage. In the Old Testament, there was no shame attached to being a concubine. Sometimes, concubines were taken from among slaves or captives. On rare occasions, a Hebrew woman might become a concubine. The life of a concubine was uncertain, though. She had few rights, lived at the mercy of the wife's vengeance, and could be sent away by the man at any time with just a gift. Any children resulting from the union between a man and his concubine were not considered equal heirs to the children of a wife, and they might be disinherited.

WHAT DOES THE BIBLE SAY ABOUT MARRIAGE AND DIVORCE?

There is not much in the Bible about the details of the marriage ceremony, but we do know that God joined the first man and woman in a marriage bond and established the family unit by that bond (Gen. 2:24–26). The man was to "leave his father and his mother, and shall cleave unto his wife: and they shall become one flesh." A man who had found a wife "findeth a good thing, and obtaineth favor of the Lord" (Prov. 18:22).

Thus, marriage was taken for granted. It was to be a holy state, the foundation of the nuclear family, and a convivial relationship of harmony, friendship, and felicity.

Besides the teaching of Jesus (Matt.19) and Paul (1 Cor. 7), the other primary passage is found in Malachi 2:16 and the surrounding verses. Though the Old Testament permits divorce, Malachi says God hates "putting away" (divorce), and is aligned against those who take that step unlawfully. Clearly, the Bible does not suggest divorce as the primary alternative to a bad marriage. Rather, Scripture called for reconciliation and a commitment to "work things out" that is not found in many other religions of the world. Marriage was a holy rite before God and included vows which, when broken, incurred God's wrath. Neither marriage nor divorce were to be entered into frivolously. Jesus told His disciples, in Matthew 19:11–12, that being a eunuch might be preferable to marriage when one considered the gravity of holy matrimony.

In the Torah, there is one passage that addresses the details of divorce (Deut. 24:1–4). From that passage, two schools developed, that of Hillel—which allowed divorce for nearly any reason—and that of Shammai—which allowed divorce only for adultery. Requiring the reason for the divorce to be stated was Moses' way of giving the wife some recourse and the opportunity for a second marriage. The certificate spelled out why the divorce was made and freed a wife from being branded as an adulterer if that was not the cause.

In the time of Jesus, the debate about divorce continued. A man could give his wife a "Certificate of Divorcement" for nearly any cause—if he found some disgrace in her, if she no longer pleased him, if she was a poor cook, and so on. However, when Jesus was asked why Moses allowed divorce, He agreed with Shammai's position and replied that Moses "permitted" divorce "because of their hardness of heart," not because God wanted them to do such a thing. He went on to say that divorce should be permitted for only one reason—adultery (see Matthew 19). And that did not require divorce if the wronged one forgave the adulterer.

Paul later added that if a believer was married to an unbeliever and the unbeliever wanted to leave—be divorced—then the believer was to let him or her go (1 Corinthians 7). However, if the unbeliever wanted to stay, Christians were not to send them away simply because they had not accepted the faith. When one was divorced because one of the partners was not a Christian, he or she could remarry. However, if two believers divorced, they were to "remain unmarried, or else be reconciled. . . ." (1 Cor. 7:11).

CHAPTER THIRTEEN

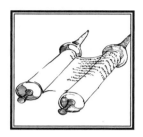

WHAT PROBLEMS DID BIBLICAL PEOPLE ENDURE?

WHAT WAS WAR LIKE IN BIBLICAL TIMES?

Throughout the Bible, stories are related about how wars were fought, won, lost, and fought again. From the beginning, threats of war intimidated the enemy. Lamech said that if Cain was avenged seven-fold, Lamech would be

147

avenged seventy-fold. God sent the Great Flood to destroy man and the world he had wrought because of the violence that reigned in the affairs of men. The first war recorded in the Bible was the war of the kings of the valley against those who paid them tribute (Gen. 14). From that point on, war was a common experience in the life of the people of Israel.

In war, anything is possible. Whole nations could be taken into slavery, or exterminated, according to the whim of the victors. The weapons of war included swords, knives, picks, hammers, pruning hooks, bows and arrows, slings, javelins, spears, battering rams, and anything else that could wound, maim, or kill. Anything could be employed in the quest for victory. Mutilation was a common means used by conquerors to intimidate cities and villages. They would select the leaders of the village and kill their sons and daughters and wives in front of the other townspeople, then skin the patriarch alive and string him up on poles. Then the village was offered the choice between surrendering as slaves to the conquering army or suffering the same fate.

There was little thought of soldiers versus civilians in the struggle. All men over age twenty were considered acting or potential soldiers, and they were killed or inducted into the conquering army on the spot. Commanders were adept at military strategies—ambush, feint, raid, surprise attack, flanking movements, forays, and other tactics. The spoils went to the victors. When his soldiers argued about the spoils, David decreed they should be equally divided by those who fought and those who watched the baggage (1 Samuel 30). On occasion, one army challenged another to a duel between their respective champions, which was how David vanquished Goliath.

In Israel, war was considered an act of God. Frequently, warriors were led into battle by priests carrying the ark of the covenant. Prophets were consulted by kings about possible victory, and King Saul even went to a medium before the last battle of his life, seeking counsel about its outcome. When the trumpet was blown in Israel, all the young and old men gathered to fight the enemy. Even God showed no mercy in the battle of Jericho when He ordered Israel into war and told them that all in that city must die—God's people must slaughter every man, woman, and child.

Right to the end of the New Testament, wars are fought. Revelation states that the war that ends our world will be Armageddon, when the armies of the world will try to wrest control of the world from Jesus Christ.

WHAT HEALTH PROBLEMS DID THE PEOPLE HAVE?

A multitude of diseases and illnesses afflicted people, sometimes as specific judgments by God, sometimes as the natural consequence of sinful actions and sometimes just in the natural course of events. Leprosy, of which Jesus healed so many during His ministry, was common, as were syphilis, smallpox, scabies, and scurvy. When Job broke out in running boils, it might have been a form of smallpox.

Bubonic plague broke out once among the Philistines when they stole the ark of the covenant (1 Sam. 5). They attributed it to a disease carried by the mice and made little golden figures of the mice, but these talismans had no effect.

Consumptive diseases were also common: tuberculosis, typhoid fever, malaria, dysentery. Various worms could infiltrate and take up residence in the body, afflicting it with an issue of pus, a "wasting away," or other sickness.

There were many other diseases that Jesus confronted: dropsy (probably modern edema), dumbness, deafness, blindness caused by glaucoma and congenital infections, lameness, withered hands, and paralysis of the lower limbs. Many of these diseases were healed by divine power, either by Jesus Himself or by His disciples and apostles. But in some cases, there was no healing.

WHAT ABOUT DEMONIC POSSESSION?

The only biblical case of demonic possession or oppression where we know the cause is that of King Saul. In 1 Samuel 16:14, the Spirit of God left the king and an "evil spirit from the Lord" terrorized him. It was at that point that David was called in to play soothing music. It's clear that the demonic oppression came about because God was disciplining King Saul for his disobedience in several matters.

In other cases, mostly in the New Testament Gospels, demonic possession is related without giving any history of the matter. One father said a boy had a demon who caused him to fall into both fire and water (Matt. 17:14–18), and this appeared to have occurred since he was young.

How does demonic possession happen? Rank disobedience to God seems to invite it. Opening oneself up to the presence of demons through various occult practices—divination, astrology, channeling (practicing as a medium), or witchcraft—is considered "trafficking in demons" that might bring the evil forces into one's soul. Jesus told His disciples in Matthew 12:43–45 that when a man becomes free of a demon and does not put his trust in God, that demon goes out and finds seven more demons even more lethal than himself, and they come back and occupy the man, leaving "the last state of that man worse than the first."

Jesus normally cast out demons with a word. He would say, "Begone," and they were gone. On occasion, He sent them into other subjects. The Gadarene demoniacs, one of whom was possessed by a demon named Legion, because "they were many," met Jesus as He walked by the tombs. The demons shrieked in horror when they realized the demoniacs had cast themselves at Jesus' feet. The demons pleaded that if He were to cast them out, He might send them into the swine feeding on the hill. Jesus complied, and 2,000 pigs rushed down the hill into the sea and drowned.

Jesus passed this authority to the disciples. It appears that they cast out demons the same way, though on one occasion they failed (see Mark 9). Jesus said that those were demons that only came out by "prayer and fasting."

Christians are not meant to fear demons. John wrote, "Greater is He that is in you, than he that is in the world" (1 John 4:4). Thus, while we're to be aware of demons and their power, we are to recognize that every believer under submission to Christ has His authority to overcome them.

WHAT KINDS
OF PLAGUES STRUCK?

Plagues happened for specific reasons. The Philistines were smitten with something resembling the bubonic plague for taking the ark of the covenant and trying to keep it (1 Sam. 6). How extensive the devastation was, we do not know, but it was great enough to convince the Philistines to return the ark to Israel.

David experienced a plague brought about by his own arrogant disobedience of "numbering" the fighting men in Israel. In 2 Samuel 24, we see that God offered David three options as discipline for his disobedience. He chose a pestilence for three days because it was better to fall into the hands of God than into the hands of his enemies. The pestilence killed 70,000 men and presumably many more women and children.

In another case, an angel of the Lord brought a plague upon the armies of Sennacherib as they besieged Jerusalem (2 Kings 19) and killed 185,000 soldiers. Herodotus, the historian, wrote that a plague came upon them, introduced by rats, possibly a very fast-acting bubonic plague.

The plagues mentioned in Scripture all came about by divine intervention. No plagues simply happened without some divine explanation. Ordinarily, any "act of God" was viewed for what it was, a true act committed by God.

WHAT HAPPENED DURING TIMES OF FAMINE?

In the Bible, famine happens to God's purpose. When famine struck, people moved on, looking for different lands where food was available. Jacob sent ten of his sons to Egypt because they heard that grain was abundant there. Joseph had warned Pharaoh of seven years of plenty and then seven years of famine. Joseph, who interpreted the dream that God gave Pharaoh, became prime minister and engineered the vast program to store the grain for the bad years. It was by this means that God moved Jacob and his family to Egypt for their incubation as a nation.

The tools by which famine occur are many. Locusts could decimate the crops of a vicinity and leave the people without resources for the winter. Drought could ravage the land, leaving it dry and parched and unsuitable for growing anything. Other plagues might attack the crops or beasts as they did in Egypt during the ten plagues of Moses. Other famines occurred throughout biblical history, sometimes with no explanation and sometimes with divine explanations. Jesus predicted that in the end days there would be numerous famines raging in the world (Matt. 24:7).

WHAT DO WE KNOW
ABOUT THE JEWISH PEOPLE
AND SLAVERY?

For people in biblical times, slavery was an accepted institution. The Bible does not judge slavery, but strived to institute laws for the just treatment of slaves. Under Roman law, slaves had no rights or recourse.

In their history, Jewish people had been both slaves and slave holders. In several periods of Jewish history, entire tribes seemed to become enslaved, then find their way to freedom. The Bible relates how Egypt enslaved the resident Hebrew population in the years following the death of prime minister Joseph. We don't know exactly how long that took, but a king arose "who did not know Joseph," and the people who once were honored guests in the land of Goshen became despised slaves until God terrified Pharaoh with a visitation of deathly plagues, and Moses led the people out of Egypt toward the Promised Land.

There were times recorded in the book of Judges that Israel suffered attacks and incursions that led to slavery, but these were infrequent and not wholesale national enslavement. Rich Jews often owned slaves, and a destitute Jewish man could sell himself or his family into slavery, but only for a term of seven years (Exod. 21:1-7).

Two catastrophic events though led to the wholesale disruption or enslavement of the people of Israel. The Assyrians captured the Northern Kingdom of the Jews in 722 B.C., and many Jewish captives were enslaved. Tens of thousands of people were uprooted from their homes, relocated into Assyria and never seen again.

The Southern Kingdom, Judah, also suffered enslavement just over 130 years later at the hands of the Babylonians in 586 B.C., but they returned to their lands as a free people seventy years later when the Babylonians were defeated by the Persians.

WHAT WAS LIFE LIKE
FOR A SLAVE?

The Bible did not forbid slavery but attempted to provide religious law and direction to insure the safekeeping and care of a slave. Unfortunately, these laws were not always followed or enforced. The words of the prophets sometimes condemn the institution of slavery in an effort to draw people's attention to the true laws.

The quality of life as a slave depended on the master. A good master could give a slave a humane life, comfortable domestic arrangements, an education, and even status (if your master had high social position). Slaves of less well-to-do masters, or small-minded masters who sought to exploit their slaves, could suffer greatly at their hands. God forbade Jews to mistreat their slaves, but such laws were not always enforced. Many people who were forced into slavery craved freedom and were advised by the Apostle Paul to seek it (1 Cor. 7:21–22).

But Paul also advised slaves to bide their time and render a good return to their masters, to serve them as if they were serving Christ Himself, until they had served out their agreement with their master (Eph. 6:5–8; 1 Tim. 6:1–2). They were commanded not to grumble about their condition and literally to make the most of it, recognizing that God promised special rewards to those who suffered.

CHAPTER FOURTEEN

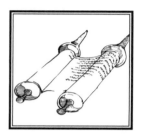

HOW WERE BIBLICAL PEOPLE GOVERNED?

WHO WERE THE RULERS?

The Bible relates how Israel went through many forms of leadership as God tried to establish equitable and fair governments for the people. In the days of Abraham, Israel was a patriarchal society. The "patriarch"—"father is king"—ruled the family. This lasted from the time of Abraham until Israel's sojourn in Egypt, where eventually the Israelites were enslaved.

When Moses became the leader of the Hebrew people, through God's will he established a new form of government. Moses appointed leaders who had responsibility over groups of citizens numbering by the thousands, hundreds, fifties, and tens. These leaders settled disputes and passed the commands from on high. It was an effective system that freed Moses to lead the people to find their way, through God, out of slavery.

When the people finally settled in the promised land, judges became the rulers, though they did not so much rule as gather together armies to defeat Israel's enemies. A pattern was established in which Israel would disobey God by worshiping idols. This led to God's discipline that arrived in the form of incursions by other nations into Israelite territory. Often Israel was beaten, marauded, and enslaved. Repentant, the people would cry out to God for relief, and He would send them a judge who would defeat the enemy and bring back freedom and comfort to the people.

During the reign of the last judge, Samuel, the people solicited God for a king. They wanted to be like the nations that surrounded them. God selected a king through Samuel. His name was Saul. Saul proved to be a disobedient, careless ruler whom God ultimately rejected. In the process, a new king was selected—David.

With kingly leadership, the nation of Israel flourished. But after the death of King Solomon, a descendant of David, the north rebelled and ten tribes seceded from Israel, becoming the Northern Kingdom of Israel. Kings from the line of David remained in the south and ruled two tribes—Judah and Benjamin—while in the north, whoever fought their way into power ruled the land. Eventually the tribes of the Northern Kingdom were captured and displaced by the Assyrians. The tribes of the Southern Kingdom lasted a little longer, but were driven into exile and slavery by the Babylonians in 586 B.C. Seventy years later, when Persia conquered the Babylonians, the tribes returned to Judea, free, but subject to Persian rule. The Persians appointed governors to rule over the Jewish people, beginning with Nehemiah, a Jew living in Persia who was held in regard by the Persian king.

Around 325 B.C., Alexander the Great rose to power and conquered Persia. When he died, his kingdom was divided into four parts and Judea became a possession of the Ptolemies in Egypt. In 198 B.C., Antiochus III, the Great, defeated Egypt and took possession of Judea for Syria. He was later defeated by the Romans in 190 B.C. He then lost control of Asia Minor, but his family continued to rule over Judea. Antiochus IV—sometimes called Epiphanes—attempted to stamp Greek philosophy and culture on the Jews. This led to his sacrifice of a pig on the altar in the main temple in Jerusalem. A revolt broke out in 168 B.C. and the Maccabees eventually gained power. In 165 B.C., Judas Maccabaeus succeeded in cleansing the Temple, and the Feast of Lights (Hanukkah) was initiated and celebrated by all Jews.

The Maccabees, also called Hasmoneans, reigned until 34 B.C., when Herod the Great succeeded in wresting control of Judea from them and reigned as king under the authority of the Romans. He was king when Jesus was born. Herod's progeny reigned later as governors, and it was Herod Antipas who was in office when Jesus was crucified.

HOW DID RULERS
COME TO POWER?

By any means they could—sometimes by normal accession, father to son; sometimes by an overthrow of the previous ruler by someone stronger; sometimes by being placed on a throne by other conquerors as revealed above.

WHO WERE THE PATRIARCHS
AND WHAT DID THEY DO?

Normally, we think of the patriarchs as being Abraham, Isaac, Jacob, and their sons and grandsons who ruled among Israel's families.

WHO WERE THE JUDGES?

The judges were spiritual or military leaders. When Israel failed to obey God during the period after the conquest of Canaan under Joshua, God disciplined them by sending marauders into the land to pillage, plunder and kill. This led to Israel's cry to God for mercy, which prompted God to raise up a judge. The judge had the power to lead, organize, and raise an army. A judge would defeat the enemies who had infiltrated the land and would rule by judging the people, settling disputes, and governing. It was a loose form of government, giving the people a great deal of individual freedom, but it was considered a theocracy—God was the real ruler.

The exploits of some of the various judges are recorded in the Book of Judges in the Old Testament. There we see such people as Deborah leading the defeat of Sisera, the general of the King of Hazor's army. Other judges were Gideon, Samson and Samuel, the prophet who anointed both King Saul and later King David as rulers of Israel.

WHY DID ISRAEL SPLIT UNDER KING REHOBOAM?

King Solomon exacted a heavy tax and labor toll on Israel to fund his building projects. When he died and Rehoboam became king, the northern tribes under Jeroboam wanted to know if he was going to be a taskmaster like Solomon. Rehoboam consulted with the elders who told him to ease up. Then he listened to the young men who told him to be even tougher. He told Jeroboam, "My little finger shall be thicker than my father's loins" (1 Kings 12:10). In other words, "I'll be a hundred times worse than Solomon ever was." So Jeroboam rebelled and took the whole northern kingdom with him.

WHO WAS THE ONE WOMAN TO RULE JUDAH?

Athaliah. She was married to Jehoram and was the daughter of the wicked couple, Ahab and Jezebel. When her son Ahaziah was killed in battle, she took the throne. She tried to wipe out the whole line of David in the process, but she missed one person. Joash, while still a baby, was hidden by the high priest and raised by him. Eventually, the elders and priests saw that Joash was restored to power and Athaliah was killed.

WHO WAS THE GREATEST KING IN SCRIPTURE?

Jewish tradition points to King David. The reasons are that he was a champion warrior, defeating such opponents as Goliath. His exploits take up half of the book of 1 Samuel and all of 2 Samuel. He expanded Israel's territory to its greatest size. He composed a multitude of Psalms, which were considered the songbook of Israel. And although he committed terrible sins, he later repented and won God's forgiveness. It was for this reason that David was sometimes called "a man after God's own heart" (1 Samuel 13:14).

WHAT IS THE WISDOM OF SOLOMON?

King David named his second son by Bathsheba, Solomon. While David is considered the greatest king in Scripture, Solomon gained great recognition as a wise and just ruler who brought the nation of Israel to great prosperity. He instituted tremendous building campaigns and built a fabulous palace beyond compare and a temple to God so magnificent that it was considered one of the seven wonders of the ancient world. When he was first king, God came to him in a dream and offered him a gift: he could have anything he requested—riches, power, anything. He chose wisdom and God, because of this excellent choice, gave him riches and power as well. He was known far and wide for his kingly wisdom.

WHEN DID ROME CONQUER ISRAEL?

The Romans under Pompey defeated the Syrians in 63 B.C. They consolidated their empire in the east at that point and took control of Palestine. Pompey appointed Hyrcanus to rule over an "ethnarchy" that included Galilee, Judea, Samaria, and Perea.

WHO WERE THE RULERS IN JESUS' DAY?

Jesus was born around 5 B.C., close to the end of the reign of Herod the Great. When Herod died in 4 B.C., his empire was divided among his three sons: Archelaus took Judea and Idumea, which was formerly called Edom, the land to the east of Judea by the Dead Sea. Philip took Iturea, which was northeast of Palestine on the other side of the Jordan River. Herod Antipas received Galilee and Perea, a small parcel of land east of the Jordan, opposite Samaria and Judea.

Herod Antipas, the one Jesus referred to as "that fox," reigned in Galilee from 4 B.C. until A.D. 39. Various intrigues led to the demise of Archelaus in Judea and the appointment of Roman governors in his place. Pontius Pilate was the Roman governor in charge at the time of Jesus' death. He sent Jesus to Herod Antipas, who sent Him back to Pilate during Jesus' trial. It was this event which sealed the friendship between Pilate and Antipas.

WHO WERE THE PHARISEES?

Some scholars believe the Pharisees were formed as a result of the Maccabean revolt of 165 B.C. It's not clear, but by the time of Jesus, there were three main groups in Judaism: the rigorously observant Pharisees, the politically minded Sadducees, and the ascetic Essenes. By far, the Pharisees were the most influential among the masses.

The name "Pharisee" means "separatists" or "separated ones." They were dedicated to a strict adherence to the Law of Moses, both written and oral.

Some Pharisees opposed Jesus initially because they believed He broke the Sabbath by healing and attending those in need. Jesus defended His actions by arguing that, if a lamb falls into a pit on the Sabbath, won't his master take him out and save him? But that did not satisfy His critics.

HOW WERE LEGAL DECISIONS MADE?

According to the blueprint in the Bible, Israel was to have a double system of courts: Judges were appointed to handle civil and criminal cases, and priests to handle religious matters. All lawsuits and other matters were to be brought before the judge, and the people involved were to represent themselves. The judge would hear the complaint and the defense and then make a ruling. Anyone who refused to abide by the ruling of the court could be executed.

In serious matters such as murder, a person could not be convicted unless there were at least two corroborating eyewitnesses. A convicted murderer would be executed by stoning, either by the victim's family, by people designated by the court, or by a group of people gathered for that purpose.

Over time, this system changed, because of both internal evolution and imposition from foreign rulers. The court system had several layers of lower courts and one could appeal to higher authority (Deut. 1:15–16). Cases were appealed only when a lower judge could not reach a decision.

WHAT RIGHTS DID ROMAN CITIZENS ENJOY?

Roman citizenship was an important, powerful privilege. It could be obtained by a decree from the emperor on the basis of service or location, or for a sum of money. People could purchase Roman citizenship, but more often it was a birthright passed from father to son. Paul was born a Roman citizen.

Roman citizens, wherever they dwelled, had all the rights and privileges of those who lived in Rome. They could appeal to Caesar in certain special matters when they did not receive satisfaction in lower courts. They were also preserved from having to undergo embarrassing or painful punishments such as scourging or crucifixion. They were considered free within the parameters of the Roman empire and could travel, buy, sell, and conduct business freely and without being hampered. Often they were free from having to pay the taxes that non-citizens were required to pay.

Paul twice invoked his Roman citizenship to escape harrowing circumstances. In Acts 16:35–40, after being whipped and jailed in Philippi, Paul informed the people involved that he was a Roman. This sent them into a state of fear, realizing that to do such things to a Roman carried a high penalty, and the local police sent an appeal to Paul to leave quietly. He immediately told them that they'd have to come and appeal to him in person. This they did, and Paul left.

In the second case, Paul was jailed in Jerusalem for taking non-Jews into the temple. When the Roman commander took Paul into custody and was about to have the apostle scourged, Paul informed him he was a Roman citizen (Acts 22:22–29). Paul was immediately released unharmed. The next day, Paul appeared before the Sanhedrin and presented a defense that led to his being shipped off to Caesarea. In the next few weeks, Paul appeared before various leaders—Felix and then Festus—and in Acts 25:8–12, finally, as was the right of any Roman citizen, he appealed to Caesar. Paul was sent to Rome.

HOW WERE LAWS MADE?

For people of Jewish faith, the book of the Law—the five books of Moses—spelled out the laws that governed their spiritual and domestic lives. Under different rulers, though, the laws of the conquering countries came to bear. Thus, the Jews had their own laws for religious matters and another legal system that meshed their civil laws with those of the ruling state.

DID THEY HAVE
A DEATH PENALTY?

Yes. The biblical form of execution was stoning. In this circumstance, the accused stood in the center of a circle of his accusers as they picked up large stones and threw them at him until he died.

In Roman times, the official form of execution for a criminal was crucifixion.

DID BIBLICAL PEOPLE
PAY TAXES?

From the earliest times, taxes have been demanded by chieftains, governors, kings, and rulers of all kinds. When Moses instituted the law, all Israelite men were required to pay a yearly poll tax, which was a half-shekel for the maintenance of the tabernacle and theocratic worship. By the time of Solomon, taxation and forced work were so hard and cruel that the ten northern tribes rebelled at Solomon's death and refused to continue payment.

Over the years, rulers required tribute money to be raised by the king through taxes; many people felt they were literally "taxed to death."

By the time of Greek and then Roman rule, a new method of taxation was instituted. The Romans farmed out taxation powers to the highest bidder. People like Zaccheus and Matthew probably paid huge sums to the government to gain the right to tax in their district. After buying the rights to a certain area, a tax collector could attempt to collect as much money as he could from those under him, who would then tax the people right down to the common man. There were several different taxes levied, including tolls for transporting goods by land or by sea. Usually, the tax was five percent of the purchase price of normal goods, and up to 12 and a half percent for luxury items. However, all tax gatherers had men over them and under them. They paid the person over them and then taxed the man under them at a slightly higher percentage than they'd paid. Many of the lower-level tax collectors, called "publicans," were Jewish. Jews considered publicans to be traitors because they were working for the Romans and extorting money from their own people.

Agricultural taxes and census taxes were also farmed out to lower-level tax collectors. All in all, the system worked well, but the people in it were despised. Jesus had hard words for tax collectors too, linking them with harlots on the lower rungs of humanity (Matt. 9:10 and 21:31). Matthew the disciple was a publican.

Taxes were used to support the government, build roads, equip soldiers for the defense of the realm, erect temples and other municipal building projects. But often taxation seemed to the taxpayer a burden beyond bearing.

CHAPTER FIFTEEN

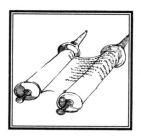

WHERE ARE THE PLACES IN THE BIBLE?

WHERE IS THE HOLY LAND?

Called "Holy" because it was land separated for God and His use, the Holy Land was the land of Israel, which included Judea, Samaria, and Galilee. The land given to Abraham by God extended from the Nile to the Euphrates Rivers, (from modern Egypt to Iraq). But God's people occupied only a small part of that area (Gen. 15:18-21). From the time of Roman conquest in A.D. 135 to 1948, on maps this area has been called Palestine.

WHERE WAS THE
GARDEN OF EDEN?

The Book of Genesis says that Eden was located among four rivers—the Pishon, which flowed around the land of Havilah; the Gihon, which wound through the land of Cush; and the Tigris and Euphrates, which, as we know today, begin in the mountains of modern Turkey and flow through Syria and Iraq to the head of the Persian Gulf. Because there is no record of where the biblical rivers Pishon and Gihon ran, no one can be sure of Eden's exact location, though it would appear that it must have been somewhere in the Middle East along the Fertile Crescent in the Tigris-Euphrates river system.

WHERE WAS THE TOWER
OF BABEL?

The Bible relates that this tower was built on the plain of Shinar, though it is not now known where Shinar is located. Throughout the Middle East and especially the region known in ancient times as Mesopotamia, many towers have been discovered by archaeologists. Most of these ruins are house towers, called "ziggurats." However, the Tower of Babel was a simple tower that stood alone.

WHERE WERE SODOM
AND GOMORRAH?

It is not known precisely where these cities were located, though most scholars place them on the southern coast of the Dead Sea, possibly in an area now submerged. But with destruction on the scale related in the Bible, little evidence would remain.

WHAT IS THE DOME
OF THE ROCK?

The "rock" is so named because it is believed this is the rock where Abraham was called to sacrifice his son, Isaac (Gen. 22). Because Abraham is sacred to Jews, Christians, and Moslems, the Dome of the Rock, located in present-day Jerusalem, is viewed as a sacred religious place for all three religions. For the Moslems, it is the most sacred of their sites because they also believe the rock is the site at which Mohammed, their prophet, ascended into heaven.

The Moslems built a shrine on the spot between A.D. 685 and 691, by the caliph 'Abh al-Malik ibn Marwan as a shrine for pilgrims. It is built in Jerusalem, on the site of what was once Solomon's magnificent temple. It is sometimes called the "Mosque of Omar."

WHERE WAS ABRAHAM BURIED?

Abraham purchased the cave of Machpelah from Ephron (Gen. 23) and was buried there at the age of 175 (Gen. 25:7–10). He was "an old man, and full of years" meaning he had had a great and blessed life filled with joyous and happy days.

Today a Mosque stands over the burial site, and entrance to the grave is forbidden. Sarah, Isaac, Rebekah, Leah, and Jacob are also buried there. It was located in a field near Hebron, located 19 miles southwest of Jerusalem in modern Israel.

WHERE IN EGYPT WERE THE ISRAELITES HELD IN SLAVERY?

They were captive in the land of Goshen, the northeast section of the Nile delta region. Because the area was well watered by the Nile delta, it was excellent for growing crops and raising sheep, goats, and cattle, which the Israelites had in abundance.

WHERE IS THE WILDERNESS
IN WHICH THE JEWS WANDERED?

Probably the Sinai Peninsula, then northeast to Transjordan. The Old Testament relates that the Jews were in the "wilderness" for forty years—from their escape from Egypt under the leadership of Moses until they began the conquest of the land of Canaan under Joshua's leadership. Their wanderings are recorded in Numbers 33, including all the places they camped.

ON WHAT MOUNTAIN DID GOD GIVE
MOSES THE TEN COMMANDMENTS?

The mountain was called Mount Sinai in Exodus 19:20, and sometimes it's also called Horeb. The exact location is unclear, but many people believe this is Jebel Musa (Mountain of Moses) and Ras Safsaf, a ridge with two peaks. One peak is 6,540 feet and the other is 7,363 feet.

WHERE IS CANAAN?

This is the location of the Promised Land to which God led Moses and his people. It was occupied by Canaanites before God's people conquered it. While the nation Canaan no longer exists, Jericho, one of the most ancient cities in the world, still flourishes.

Modern Jericho is located five miles west of the Jordan River and seven miles north of the Dead Sea. The city of Jericho of the Old Testament was located about one mile northwest of the modern town on a mound, called Tell el-Sultan, which has been much excavated by archaeologists.

As related in Joshua 6, the city was surrounded by the forces of Joshua as the first stronghold the tribe of Israel approached in their promised land. It was considered so formidable that the Israelites needed divine help to fell it. Israelites marched around the walled city for seven days, once each day. On the seventh day, they marched around it seven times. At the end, they blew trumpets and shouted. The walls, as the song says, came tumbling down.

Archaeologists thought they had unlatched the mystery of Jericho when John Garstang dug there from 1930 to 1936. He found two walls, an inner wall measuring twelve feet thick, and an outer wall, six feet thick, that had fallen outward. Inside the compound was enough char and rubble to indicate that the city had been burned. He dated it as Joshua's conquest around 1400 B.C. Later, in the 1950s, Kathleen Kenyon did excavations to prove or disprove Garstang's theory. She ended up dating the destruction at about 3000 B.C., and said it was not Joshua's conquest. The mound has been ravaged so much by time and people scraping away the ruins that little is left.

Thus, the mystery remains. Few scholars today believe that Garstang's Jericho is the one of biblical record. Nonetheless, built 5,000 years before the birth of Abraham, Jericho remains as one of the world's oldest cities.

WHERE WAS
SOLOMON'S TEMPLE?

Solomon built his magnificent temple in Jerusalem. It was destroyed in 586 B.C. and everything of value was taken to Babylon by King Nebuchadnezzar. The temple was located on the site now occupied by the Dome of the Rock.

WHERE WERE THE LANDS
OF THE QUEEN OF SHEBA?

The Queen's visit is spoken of in 1 Kings 10:1–13 in which she claimed that "the half was not told me" of Solomon's wealth and wisdom. She was a Sabean, perhaps descended from Abraham through Jokshan, his son by Keturah whom he married after Sarah's death. Her people may have been a nomadic people, often trading in precious stones, incense, and slaves. Her lands were found in southern Arabia, present-day Saudi Arabia.

WHERE WAS BABYLONIA?

Located between the banks of the Tigris and Euphrates Rivers in southern Mesopotamia. The empire grew and diminished over the 2,500 years of biblical history.

The Hanging Gardens of Babylon, one of the seven wonders of the ancient world, were built by King Nebuchadnezzar to comfort his wife and remind her of her mountainous home and its gardens. They were in Babylon near the palace.

WHY IS JERUSALEM
SO IMPORTANT IN THE BIBLE?

Jerusalem was known as the "Holy City" and the "City of God" in ancient times and was considered the capital of Israel. It was also known as the City of David because David conquered it and was the first Hebrew king to make it his capital.

It was called "Jerusalem," which meant city of peace. There the kings in the great golden age of Israel reigned on the throne of David. There, Jesus died, rose and ascended, and performed many of His miraculous acts. He taught there in the temple and gave us many of His greatest words there. It is, above all, the capital of God's kingdom on earth.

NOTES

1. David Wallechinsky and Irving Wallace, *The People's Almanac*, 1286-87.

2. Ibid.

3. Material adapted from H.L. Willmington, *Willmington's Book of Bible Lists*, 122-123.

4. Material adapted from H.L. Willmington, *Willmington's Book of Bible Lists*, 260-263.

5. Merrill C. Tenney, *Pictorial Bible Dictionary*, 281.

BIBLIOGRAPHY

Archer, Gleason L., Jr. *A Survey of Old Testament Introduction.* Chicago, Illinois: Moody Press, 1964.

Bruce, F. F. *New Testament History.* Garden City, New York: Anchor Books, 1972.

Davis, John J. *Moses and the Gods of Egypt.* Grand Rapids, Michigan: Baker Book House, 1971.

Douglas, J. D., gen. ed. *The New International Dictionary of the Christian Church.* Grand Rapids, Michigan: The Zondervan Corporation, 1978.

Edersheim, Alfred *The Life and Times of Jesus the Messiah.* Grand Rapids, Michigan: Wm. B. Eerdmans Company, n.d.

Edersheim, Alfred. *Sketches of Jewish Social Life.* Grand Rapids, Michigan: Wm. B. Eerdmans Company, 1974.

Edersheim, Alfred. *The Temple.* Grand Rapids, Michigan: Wm. B. Eerdmans Company, 1958.

Fergusen, Everett, ed. *Encyclopedia of Early Christianity.* New York: Garland Publishing, Inc., 1990.

Gromacki, Robert G. *New Testament Survey.* Grand Rapids, Michigan: Baker Book House, 1974.

Hiebert, D. Edmond. *An Introduction to the New Testament, Volume II.* Chicago, Illinois: Moody Press, 1977.

Holmes, Michael W., ed. *The Apostolic Fathers, Second Edition.* Grand Rapids, Michigan, Baker Book House, 1989.

Jones, Alexander, gen. ed. *The Jerusalem Bible.* New York: Doubleday and Company, 1968.

Kitchen, K. A. *The Bible in Its World.* Downers Grove, Illinois: InterVarsity Press, 1977.

LeTourette, Kenneth Scott. *A History of Christianity.* New York: Harper and Row, Publishers, 1953.

Moyer, Elgin S. *The Wycliffe Biographical Dictionary of the Church.* Chicago, Illinois: Moody Press, 1982.

Murphey, Cecil B., comp. *The Dictionary of Biblical Literacy.* Nashville, Tennessee: Thomas Nelson Publishers, 1989.

Packer, James I., Merrill C. Tenney and William White, Jr., eds. *The Bible Almanac.* Nashville, Tennessee: Thomas Nelson Publishers, 1980.

Shneemelcher, William, ed. *New Testament Apocrypha.* Louisville, Kentucky: Westminster/John Knox Press, 1990.

Sproul, R. C. *Knowing Scripture.* Downers Grove, Illinois: InterVarsity Press, 1977.

Tenney, Merril C., gen. ed. *The Zondervan Pictorial Bible Dictionary.* Grand Rapids, Michigan: The Zondervan Corporation, 1967.

Tenney, Merril C. *The Zondervan Pictorial Encyclopedia of the Bible.* Vol. 1–5. Grand Rapids, Michigan: The Zondervan Corporation, 1976.

Unger, Merril F. *Archaeology and the Old Testament.* Grand Rapids, Michigan: The Zondervan Corporation, 1954.

Wallechinsky, David and Irving Wallace. *The People's Almanac.* Garden City, New York: Doubleday and Company, 1975.

Wight, Fred H. *Manners and Customs of Bible Lands.* Chicago, Illinois: Moody Press, 1953.

Willmington, H. L. *Willmington's Book of Bible Lists.* Chicago, Illinois: Tyndale House Publishers, Inc., 1987.

Wood, Leon. *A Survey of Israel's History.* Grand Rapids, Michigan: The Zondervan Corporation, 1970.

ABOUT THE AUTHOR

Mark Littleton is a graduate of Colgate University and Dallas Theological Seminary. He has served both as a youth pastor and pastor, and continues his ministry today as an itinerant speaker and writer of all things factual and fabulous. He has published over thirty books on various themes and subjects, including the spiritual life, depression, time management, Bible study, and the problem of evil and suffering. He has also published novels for children, one series called *The Crista Chronicles* (published by Harvest House) and a second named *The Rocky Creek Adventures* (published by David C. Cook).

Mark has two daughters, Nicole and Alisha, who keep waiting for him to write a book about them. The family also has a cat, Beauty, who refuses to read anything Mark writes. They live in Columbia, Maryland.